FOR SURELY HE HAS FORGIVEN ME

THE POWER OF GOD'S LOVE

pamela b h victor

iUniverse, Inc.
New York   Bloomington

FOR SURELY HE HAS FORGIVEN ME
THE POWER OF GOD'S LOVE

iUniverse books may be ordered through booksellers or by contacting:

iUniverse
1663 Liberty Drive
Bloomington, IN 47403
www.iuniverse.com
1-800-Authors (1-800-288-4677)

Because of the dynamic nature of the Internet, any Web addresses or links contained in this book may have changed since publication and may no longer be valid.

ISBN: 978-1-4401-7240-3 (sc)
ISBN: 978-1-4401-7241-0 (ebk)

Printed in the United States of America

iUniverse rev. date: 11/3/2009

Contents

INTRODUCTION

Very often we use the word "dysfunction" to refer to any person or persons whose behaviour or character contradict what may be called "normal" in our society or communities; [broken homes, broken families, broken lives........ everything that affects all levels of human existence spiritually, mentally, emotionally and psychologically. A lack of peace, a downgraded way of living and a loss of dignity can all sum up a dysfunctional life. Circumstances play an all important role in all this, but "dysfunction" truly began the moment that Adam and Eve [the first parents of the human race] used their free wills to disobey and rebel against the commandment of our Creator God. Every one born into the human race since then has been dysfunctional, because sin and death entered into the world and man has been separated from God his Creator. By this we should all draw the conclusion that man has no hope whatsoever in this world except through Jesus Christ. He is the perfect sacrifice, the Holy Lamb of God, slain from the foundation of the world, the great Prince of Peace. He was sent by God the Father to cause us to function in the way which He had planned from the beginning of time. Jesus came to "redeem us from all iniquity and purify for Himself a peculiar people zealous of good works". *TITUS 2;14.* KING JAMES. As we turn our eyes upon Him, we can experience freedom and forgiveness from any dysfunctional past. He is the beginning and the ending, the first and the last; He covers every area and aspect of life and holding the keys of death and hell, Jesus promises abundant life, a new way of living and everlasting life in eternity! No one's past can determine their future and destiny when they put their trust in Him, for no one who puts their trust in Him will be disappointed. Most of what has been written on these pages has been compiled from some of my personal experiences and that of others whom I have been privileged to come in contact with and more so what I believe the Holy Spirit has helped me with in recognizing my own self and my constant need for more of Him moment by moment on this journey called life. I hope that these experiences will be helpful and applicable to everyone who reads this book, and those

pamela b h victor

who are silent sufferers from a painful past, that you too will embark on the wonderful journey of restoration and wholeness through the redemptive work of our Lord and Saviour Jesus Christ.

FOR SURELY HE HAS FORGIVEN ME

"Unto Him that loved us and washed us from our sins in His own blood, and hath made us kings and priests unto God and His Father; to Him be glory and dominion for ever and ever. **Amen."**

Revelation 1: 5,6. *King James Bible*

DEDICATION

To my children :

I love you and appreciate you so very much. I consider you as God's gifts to me and an important part of His plan for my life. I know that you have been through various hardships, trials, and mental and emotional turmoil, but I do believe that somewhere in your heart you would agree that God has always been faithful. He loves you in a way no one else can and you must allow Him to be your own personal God. He is a Father and longs for you to know and acknowledge Him as such. He is not a careless, unloving father but a Father of love, mercy and wonderful grace. Please realize that it is His will for you to know Him and to experience His great love every day of your lives. Let your heart's cry be as the apostle Paul who wrote in Philippians 3:10- "For my determined purpose is that I may know Him (that I may progressively become more deeply and intimately acquainted with Him, perceiving and recognizing and understanding the wonders of His person (more strongly and more clearly) Amplified Bible.

Wherever you have experienced pain, emptiness, loneliness and unfulfillment, reach out to Him and let His love and grace be experienced in your hearts. His mercies are new every morning. His presence fills all loneliness, and His resurrection power will lift you out of every despair and hopelessness – putting you on a pathway of peace and joy.

Since God is a loving Father – a father to the fatherless and helper to the helpless, He wants you to know that He stands ready to heal every broken wounded area of your lives. Do not submit to the foul counsel of the "father of lies", satan himself, who would promise you relief by counterfeit means offering you temporary ease from emotional pain. He does this by offering "substitutes" which can only numb the pain. His purpose is to steal, to kill and to destroy. John 10:10. Jesus called him the thief, and also the "father of lies". Do not buy into his deception, but come to your Heavenly Father through Jesus Christ His Son, Who has made it possible for us all to become His dearly loved children. Any pain or suffering you may experience in this life has already been taken care of by the sacrifice of Jesus on the cross when He spoke those words "It is finished". John 19:30. Begin with the cross, which is the place that all new life and hope begins. As you do this you will most certainly end with your crown in heaven in the Presence of the King of kings and Lord of lords. Live by the word of God, and always let it be the final authority for all of life's decisions. In this world Jesus said, you will experience trouble at various times, either brought on by yourselves through bad decisions, or through situations imposed on you by others. In a fallen world, all of these things are to be expected, but your response to negative circumstances is the key. If you respond in ways resulting in anger, resentment, rebellion and unforgiveness you will live a defeated life. Instead draw near to the Father of mercies and the God of all comfort and He will give you the grace to forgive those who have wronged you and to receive forgiveness for those you have wronged. He promises to make every thing new in it's time. Ecclesiastes 3:3. When you believe the fact that God really does love you, and you respond to His love you will walk in freedom from becoming a victim of emotional pain and trauma. You can choose to be a victim or a victor in this life because problems will always arise. You may be lied upon, misunderstood, abandoned, rejected or wounded by the words and actions of others. Please run to Jesus and let Him dispel all fears by His loving counsel, wash away all pain by His tender mercy and give you grace to stand until victory is experienced. Always walk in forgiveness letting it be a way of life. This is not a "walk in the park" or an "overnight remedy", but by God's grace He will enable you and teach you so that you could be all that He wants you to be.

I truly love you with the unconditional love of God.

Isaiah 43:18-19

"Remember ye not the former things, neither consider the things of old. Behold, I will do a new thing: now it shall spring forth; shall ye not know it? I will even make a way in the wilderness, and rivers in the desert."

KING JAMES BIBLE

There are many people, including precious born again Christians who have been emotionally wounded somewhere in their past or who have felt that they were directly responsible for the pain and suffering in the lives of others. They continue to carry the pain of their experiences hidden deeply within their memories. Some have embarked in the arena of unwise choices, and are plagued with troubled personalities, loaded with guilt and have not been fully able to receive the Love of God. There seems to be a mental ascent of God's mercy, love and forgiveness, but somehow this has not fully penetrated into the deep areas of the memories and emotions where open wounds reside with excruciating pain. These wounds can in themselves be covered with many temporary bandages and a scar can be the result while they go on through life, but if the root level of the problem is not dealt with and severed, there will always be a living connection to these painful issues. Satan's snare is to keep us in the cycle of looking back into the past; bringing constant reminders of our sins and failures, and even of the people who were involved in those troubling circumstances. Emotional bondage is therefore the tragic result.

God has made the provision and availability through the Precious Blood of Jesus for us to receive full forgiveness as His children. This is also true for anyone who would ever call upon the Name of the Lord Jesus Christ, making Him the Lord of their lives. Our consciences can be cleansed from "dead works and lifeless observances to serve the living God". Hebrews 9:14. *AMP. Amplified bible.* While keeping our focus on the past in such negative ways, we tend to forget the goodness of God and His plan for our lives. We forget His promises and His Covenant, and our understanding of Calvary and what was accomplished there becomes blurred. Jesus is ***now*** our resurrected High Priest Who sits at the Right Hand of the Father interceding on our behalf. Hebrews 3:1 We must consider and remember Jesus and His love for us. The Blood of Jesus has given to us a completely new beginning. In His boundless love and mercy, He foreknew these things and made complete provision for our restoration. Psalm 103:12-14. He has removed our rebellious acts as far away from us as the east is from the west. The Lord is like a father to His children, tender and compassionate to those who fear Him. For He understands how weak we are; He knows we are only dust". God wants us to know that the future He has planned for us is unhindered by anything we ever faced in the past; separate from former sins and mistakes and will not be impeded by anything concocted by the subtlety of the enemy of our souls. Jeremiah 29:11 *AMP. Amplified Bible._*

"For I know the thoughts and plans that I have for you, says the Lord, thoughts and plans for welfare and peace and not for evil, to give you hope in your final outcome".

pamela b h victor

The Blood of Jesus can give us new life and a whole new beginning even when we have missed the mark somewhere in our walk with the Lord. What He wants us to do most of all is to repent and believe in our brokenness that we are forgiven. "A broken spirit and a contrite heart He will not despise." *Psalms 51:17. AMP. Amplified Bible.*

I pray that some light will be applied to any areas of deep internal struggle, and that blessing , hope and encouragement will come to all God's people. For those who do not yet know Jesus Christ as Lord and Saviour, I pray that you will be drawn to Him by His Holy Spirit. May all those whose lives have been shattered by emotional wounds of the past find rest in the finished work of our loving Saviour. If you as a Christian have been living out a mere existence, and find it difficult to forgive or receive God's loving gift of forgiving grace due to your lingering painful past, please understand that people do things which are against God's will due to the presence of the sin nature within them .Until they have come into an experience with God's love and the knowledge of His saving grace through Jesus Christ, they are capable of some of the most despicable acts. The good news is that whenever genuine healing comes to any emotionally wounded person, they see themselves not as a victim anymore, and the abuser or wrong doer not as an enemy, but as someone loved by God and needing Him desperately. This sobering thought will help us to walk in the complete ministry of forgiveness and reconciliation as Jesus would have us to do by His Spirit and His grace.

God's loving gift of forgiving grace is free to everyone without exception or reservation. It is something we cannot earn or purchase with anything this natural world has to offer. We did not do anything to merit, or qualify for it, but because of His great love for us has He offered to us this unspeakable gift freely. "Thanks be to God for His indescribable gift!"
2 Corinthians 9:15. NIV. New International Version.

The whole point of salvation is that we are forgiven. Jesus paid the penalty for our sins, and His death covers past, present and future sins.

THE ISSUE OF RELATIONSHIPS.

Relationships always connect people together in one way or another. Perhaps you may have suffered [and most of us have] the painful experience of an absent father [a topic I would refer to a little later on], and it has left you with what I would call an "emotional or spiritual hole in your life! In your brokenness you may have found yourself comparing God to your absent father, and have developed a deep mistrust of Him. You see we all as human beings have been born into this world with certain legitimate needs, such as the need for love and affection, security, a sense of belonging and self worth or self esteem. When these needs are not met legitimately, and our search for significance seems futile, we can find ourselves setting out to accomplish meeting those very important needs in illegitimate ways all in an effort to fill the holes created by such deficits in our lives. Because so many of us, from our earliest years have experienced brokenness within the immediate circle of relationships which surrounded our lives beginning with our parents and family members, God the Father through Jesus Christ came to heal this brokeness and restore us to a right and lasting relationship with Him. Jesus connects us completely to the Father, who is not an absent Father or One who goes and comes in and out of our lives. When Jesus called His disciples, He called them to be with Him. The connection of our relationship with our Heavenly Father is through the blood of Jesus- His life, death and resurrection and ascension assures us that we have been called, chosen and made secure in this love relationship which is forever. We no longer have to worry about Him leaving, for He has given His Word over and over again that "I will never leave you or forsake you". *Hebrews 13:5* "Whosoever believeth on Him will not be ashamed." *King James Romans 9:33.* There are many who through broken relationships have sought the emotional dependency of others who are just as broken as themselves to meet their emotional needs and have found their lives still lacking in peace, joy and fulfillment. This is because God never intended for us to get our needs met from each other but through our relationship with

1

Him. He is the only source of completeness wholeness and fullness. Any true spiritual and emotional healing which we would receive, begins with the understanding of a genuine relationship with our Lord and Saviour Jesus Christ. When we are born again and are a part of this great living breathing organism called the church of whom Jesus is the Head and Bridegroom, we become His precious bride. It is just awesome to know that He can take our lives from the deepest pits of sin and shame and elevate us to such a high and lofty position! This is enough to shout a resounding Hallelujah! We have been called to belong to Jesus Christ, because God the Father loves us so dearly and has called us to be His very own. *Romans 1:6.* So wherever there has been a feeling of abandonment and insecurity, which many times causes people to wander down pathways of destruction in search for love and belonging, we all can rest assured in the integrity and outstanding validity of God's Word to us. He can be trusted! Throughout the centuries of time countless millions upon millions of lives have been forever changed through trusting in this wonderful God and Father Who offers us a most unique and honorable relationship with Him through His Son. Also important for us to realize and grasp is that God the Father is not a dictator or a controller. He does not force us into this relationship! He beacons, woos, and calls in various ways because of His great love for all, and desires passionately that we enter into this deep personal and intimate relationship with Him. He is not concerned with a flirtatious relationship, because as I mentioned before He is not going and coming in and out of our lives as so often happens in human relationships. He is a covenant keeping God, and His love and promises in our relationship with Him are binding and forever.

THE CRIES OF THE WOUNDED HEART.

"I could never do anything right, that's what they said". "How can I ever forgive him/her….. my childhood was destroyed". "I did not ask to be born, but my parents have always rejected me". "You don't know what my brother did to me when I was only six". "I went on a date, was raped and afterwards became pregnant!" "I heard my family members whispering constantly about me saying such things as "she/he would not amount to anything; if only she/he would be like the others in the family". "I ran away from home due to verbal and physical abuse and this is what I got for it". "Why was I subjected to live in a home with a father who constantly entered my room at night, and told me that he loved me and needed to prove his love for me by introducing me to sex at an early age." "I have always felt rejected so what other choice did I have?" "Being molested at such an early age has led me to a life of promiscuity". "My father physically battered my mother while we as children looked on; she eventually sought refuge in a shelter for abused women and my siblings and I were placed in foster homes! I feel so hopeless!"

On and on does the story of woe flow out from the hearts of those who have been severely wounded in their past. From the womb[where rejection can begin], or other forms of turmoil took root, the crib, the toddler, the preschooler, the tender years that follow immediately, leading into preteens and young adulthood……. The words and actions of those we have the closest interactions with through our earliest years, have either a positive or negative effect on us. The mothers, fathers, aunts, uncles, grandparents, siblings, and in some cases even temporary caregivers and teachers……everything that was seen or heard, good or bad is retained in our memories. Every experience we have had during those precious formative years with those closest to us helps to shape us for our adult future. Experiences which have been negative and painful very often predispose some to sinful responses and programmed personality patterns in direct opposition to God's divine plan for their lives.

Apart from the crisis that wounds inflicted during those early years can cause, there are also wounds that develop during a person's adult life. Some of these may involve marital separation, a child's rejection of a parent, sibling rivalry, quarrel between friends as a result of betrayal, spousal abuse.... physical or verbal, unpleasant and difficult situations in a work place, or even in a church [and yes it can happen there too], for people are often hurt and offended in the household of faith; or loss of a loving parent, or even a child sometimes leave many deeply wounded. These are some of the tragic circumstances which can present themselves to us as we live in a fallen sinful world. Some of these problems which create wounds in the adult years can cause one to live with mistrust. They can't trust anyone, preferring to fold up into a shell with an invisible sign that says "stay away from me...I'm hurting"! Some may tearfully say "I was serving God faithfully, but He let my loved one be taken away from me. How can I go on"? What has happened here? A wounded heart that is filled with pain has developed due to deep emotional wounding. This of course does not mean that one should not grieve the loss, but when it turns into an overwhelming sense of hopelessness coupled with a spirit of grief and sorrow then there needs to be some renewed sense of understanding of God's divine love and care which when revealed lifts despair and desolation. We must always remember that our emotions when enveloped with pain can move us into actions and responses that oppose the love and grace that God desires to release into our lives when we face any given situation.

The heart that knows disappointment may cry...."If God cares why is He holding out on me? Look at how long I've been waiting! Does He even care that this burden is too much for me?"

"I can't take it any more." The children of Israel actually felt that the Lord their God had hated them by bringing them out of Egyptian bondage and so murmured against Him constantly. The Bible says that they murmured and grumbled in their tents saying "because the Lord hated us, He hath brought us forth out of the land of Egypt to deliver us into the hand of the Amorites to destroy us." *Deuteronomy 1:27.* Even though the Lord was carrying them "as a man carries his son, in all the way that you went until you came to this place, yet you did not believe [trust, rely on and remain steadfast to] the Lord your God.]" *Deuteronomy 1:31. AMP.* Not understanding His love and dealings will cause us to murmur and speak against Him wrongfully, when all the while He has so much of His goodness to offer to us. God is so good that even when we fail to understand Who He really is, due to overwhelming circumstances and problems He does not just turn His back on us. He has promised never to leave us or forsake us, for He loves us with an everlasting love and stands ready to reveal Himself to us and to comfort us in ways far beyond our natural expectation. Sometimes our murmuring and failure to believe Him can cause us to come short of what He has promised us.

Now did the Lord see what happened back then? Where was He and why did He not prevent these things from happening? If these have been your questions here are some of His thoughts towards you when you think He has deserted you. "Never! Can a mother forget her nursing child? Can she feel no love for a child she has borne? But even if that were possible, I would not forget you! See, I have written your name on my hand" *Isaiah 49:15.*

Isaiah 49:15-16. NLT. New Living Translation.

"Even if my father and mother abandon me, the Lord will hold me close. *Psalm 27:10.*

In case this has slipped you due to the pain and grief which has gripped your heart you may continue to ask......"can God understand? He is up there in the heavens on His throne, I do know that He is God, but does He not realize the pain and suffering that I am now encountering"? One of my dear friends at a certain period in her life said this to me...."I think that when I pray, God puts on His pyjamas goes to sleep and continues to ignore me". This was a concept and thought which she held due to disappointment, pain and feelings that He had neglected her. She became doubtful. She genuinely loved God but was still vacillating in the area concerning His loving response to her and her desperate needs and His care. Remember that even in the valley of the shadow of death, when everything around us seems to be "dying" so to speak and we feel stuck in circumstances which do not change as we would like them to, He is still there with His rod and His staff comforting and protecting us. No one has ever made us a promise that they would never leave us or forsake us; only Jesus has made this great promise to us, which is yea and amen , and we must believe it. The failure to understand God's love and grace is present in so many of our lives and can literally cripple us hindering our true potential to serve God fully, trust Him completely and be all that He has called us to be. Have you ever stood alongside someone who was going through some sort of trauma in their lives? You did all you can to empathize regarding the situation. You prayed, believed with and for them and spent long hours at a time encouraging them and assuring them that you understood exactly what they were going through; maybe you had encountered some similar troubles and felt qualified enough to say to them "I do understand, I've been there before". I believe that most of us have had this blessed opportunity at some point in our lives.

But can we go a little further to discover with a renewed sense of hope, and a fresh revelation of someone Who is even greater than us all- Whose understanding is perfect and Who has already experienced and entered into every manner of sorrow, rejection, pain, suffering loneliness and cruelty known to humanity! One who stands ready to help us! Who has passed through death and is now alive forever. Yes, His Name is Jesus. Was any of this for Himself, on account of sin or failure on His part? NO. It was for you and me. Do your tears mean anything to Him? Do your groans in the middle of the night get His attention? Yes! "Thou tellest my wanderings; put thou my tears into thy bottle; are they not in thy book" psalms 56:8. *King James.* You must believe that they do. Here is why. "That is why we have a High Priest who has gone to heaven, *Jesus the Son of God.* Let us cling to Him and never stop trusting Him. This High Priest of ours understands our weaknesses *for He faced all of the same temptations we do, yet He did not sin.* So let us come boldly to the throne of our gracious God; there we will receive His mercy, and we will find grace to help us when we need it"

Hebrews 4:14-16. NLT. New Living Translation.

He is touched with the feeling of our infirmities.

"Why sayest thou, O Jacob, and speakest, O Israel my way is hid from the Lord, and my judgement is passed over from my God? Hast thou not known? Hast thou not heard, that the everlasting God, the Lord, the Creator of the ends of the earth, fainteth not, neither is weary? There is no searching of His understanding."

Isaiah 40:27-28.

Jesus came here in the form of a man, entered into the arena of every temptation to sin, and endured every insult and evil, the feeling of rejection, guilt and torment that humanity would ever face. He is touched with the feeling of our infirmities.

Hebrews 4:15.

In the Old Testament those chosen to be High Priest were subject to weaknesses or infirmities themselves, which caused them to understand and be able to serve and offer the necessary gifts and sacrifices for both their own sins, failures and those of the people. Their ministry was only temporary, and so in the fullness of time Jesus was sent to earth to completely identify with us in all that we would ever go through. All High Priests in the Old Testament were required to be without physical defects in order to be acceptable to God. Even the animal sacrifices had to be without blemish or defect. Jesus is referred to as the sinless spotless Lamb of God qualified to fulfill all the requirements necessary for becoming a merciful High Priest because He was without sin and never had to offer any sacrifices for Himself.

THE MINISTRY OF HIS SUFFERING

As we recall the slaps in the face the spitting, mocking, name calling and accusations hurled at Jesus during and at the end of His ministry, where He had every opportunity to yield to sin but He did not, because the Father's will was His first priority. This meant going to the cross to pay the ultimate price for our sins and the sins of the world. "Let us strip off every weight that slows us down, especially the sin that so easily hinders our progress. And let us run with endurance the race that God has set before us. We do this by keeping our eyes on Jesus, on whom our faith depends from start to finish. He was willing to die a shameful death on the cross because of the joy He knew would be His afterward. Now He is seated in the place of Highest Honor beside God's throne in heaven. Think about all He endured when sinful people did such terrible things to Him, so that you don't become weary and give up. After all, you have not yet given your lives in your struggle against sin". *Hebrews 12:1-4. NLT. New Living Translation.*

Jesus understands all our emotional problems and the anguish which come from them. Can you imagine the anguish of His sinless soul as He faced every temptation to sin which was presented to Him by the devil? He resisted him completely knowing that man's redemption was at stake. Shall we visit the Garden of Gethsemane where the devil did all he could to get Jesus not to carry out His Father's will. He prayed, He cried, while the powers of darkness assailed Him. "While Jesus was here on earth He offered prayers and pleadings with a loud cry and tears to the One Who could deliver Him out of death and God heard His prayers because of His reverence for God. *Hebrews 5:7. NLT. New living Translation.*

Jesus had sweated great drops of blood and was filled with anguish and deep distress. He told His diciples "My soul is crushed with grief to the point of death. Stay here and watch with me".

He knows and feels our anguish and grief and pain of every kind. "Then an angel from heaven appeared and strengthened Him. He prayed more fervently, and He was in such agony of spirit that His sweat fell to the ground like great drops of blood." *Luke 22:43-44. NLT. New Living Translation.*

He became so traumatized as it were that God had to dispatch an angel to strengthen Him for what was to come. Being in every respect God, He willingly condescended to become man so that He could be now a merciful High Priest Who now sits at the Father's right Hand making intercession for us. Reason being that He endured everything which we ever will experience in this life. There in Gethsemane, He fought valiantly with the prince of darkness and won the battle for us. Do you feel abandoned today? Jesus' disciples fled and abandoned Him in His hour of greatest need. Peter even denied that he ever knew Him, while Judas betrayed Him. *Mathew 26:56,69-75.* He feels and understands. *Isaiah* has given to us one of the most vivid accounts of the agony, and death of our great High priest. I believe that this account fits into every manner of pain, shame, suffering and sorrow we could ever face. *Isaiah 53:1-9.* "Who hath believed our report? And to whom is the arm of the Lord revealed? For He shall grow up before Him as a tender plant, and as a root out of dry ground: He hath no form nor comeliness; and when we shall see Him, there is no beauty that we shall desire Him. He is despised and rejected of men; a man of sorrows, and acquainted with grief: and we hid as it were our faces from Him; He was despised and we esteemed Him not. Surely He hath borne our griefs, and carried our sorrows; yet we did esteem Him stricken, smitten of God, and afflicted. But He was wounded for our transgressions, He was bruised for our iniquities: the chastisement of our peace, was upon Him; and with His stripes we are healed. All we like sheep have gone astray; we have turned every one to His own way; and the Lord hath laid on Him the iniquity of us all. He was oppressed, and He was afflicted, yet He opened not His mouth: He is brought as a Lamb to the slaughter, and as a sheep before her shearers is dumb, so He openeth not His mouth. He was taken from prison and from judgement: and who shall declare His generation? For He was cut off out of the land of the living: for the transgression of my people was He stricken. And He made His grave with the wicked, and with the rich in His death; because He had done no violence, neither was any deceit in His mouth". *King James.*

As Jesus faced the desperate angry mob on the way to Calvary, He felt all the terror that hell had to offer. Besides the spitting, the whipping, the beating and the jeering, He also suffered the sense of abandonment and separation from His Father's care and love. Have you ever felt that your prayers to God were unheard and that He had hid Himself away from you? I have and it's really daunting and depressing. You say "where are you God? Why are you so far away from me?" You feel forgotten and forsaken. Jesus had those same feelings. When the soldiers got through with the scourging, beating Him, and forcing Him to carry His own cross, the Bible says that His whole appearance was marred more than any man's, and His form beyond that of the son's of men. *Isaiah 52:14-15._* Can you imagine that He no longer looked like a human being? On that day I dare say that legions of demons in their various ranks, satan's choicest generals and leuitenants came out of their dungeons in the pit of darkness as they were all summoned to Jerusalem. Along with satan himself they unleashed every sinful wicked assault on our Blessed Lord and Saviour The poison of sin in all it's ramifications along with every curse and deception which it had destructively held mankind in bondage ever since the days of Adam and Eve, was being placed on our blessed Lord. Death was present along with hell. No wonder His being was so marred beyond any other human being. So awful was the sight that the Father literally hid His face away from His Son. God did not leave Him but Jesus nevertheless felt the abandonment for that precise moment. He cried out on the cross "my God, my God why hast thou forsaken me." Yes He feels. He is touched with all our infirmities, because He entered into all our experiences and felt what it was like. He is <u>now</u> exalted to the Father's right Hand, but He has not left us without help. He has sent to us the Holy Spirit, the Comforter to assist us in all our infirmities or weaknesses. He told His disciples "But I will send you the Counselor - the Spirit of truth. He will come to you from the Father and will tell you all about Me." *John 15:26. NLT. New Living Translation.* The Apostle Paul under the influence of the Holy Spirit wrote "And the Holy Spirit helps us in our distresses. For we don't even know what we should pray for, nor how we should pray. But the Holy Spirit prays for us with groanings that cannot be expressed in words. And the Father Who knows all hearts knows what the Spirit is saying, for the Spirit pleads for us believers in harmony with God's own will. And we know that God causes everything to work together for the good of those who love God and are called according to His purpose for them". *Romans 8:26-28. NLT. New Living Translation.*

Seeing then that we have not been abandoned, left alone or rejected should we not proceed to discover that God's plan of salvation for us did not end with us only being born again and having a redeemed spirit, but also includes the restoration of our souls [our minds, which must be reprogrammed and renewed, our emotions which were damaged and marred even from as far back as the fall and became even more damaged through several painful situations through life being fully healed and restored and our wills aligning with His will for us. Our bodies will one day be fully redeemed and be in a glorified state, but while we live here on this earth, they serve as the outer house for our spirits and our souls. Isn't God our Creator just awesome? Only He could devise such a wonderful plan and create us to be this marvelous workmanship. We truly are fearfully and wonderfully made.

Because Jesus has been resurrected from the tomb and lives forever, we have the promise of newness of life through His resurrection power now and in the eternity of eternities.

HOW BADLY DO YOU REALLY WANT TO BE HEALED?

How desperate are you to be healed and made whole? There are two very familiar examples in the Bible to which I would make brief references. First of all the man at the Pool of Bethsaida. He was in this infirm condition for 38 years. Jesus asked him one question. "Would you like to get well? *John 5:6. NLT. New Living Translation.* His excuse was that everyone got into the pool when the water was stirred up before he was able to get in. He complained that no one helped him. Thirty eight years he remained in this helpless condition. Jesus told him "stand up, pick up your sleeping mat and walk." Verse 8 of the same chapter. He showed no great desperation to be healed. The other example was the woman with the issue of blood. She visited several doctors in an effort to be rid of her condition, but instead of getting better she became worst. This went on for 12 years until she heard about Jesus, and in desperation she decided to press her way through the crowds of people who were thronging Him so that she would receive her breakthrough and she did. Her decision was to touch the hem of His garment as she kept saying to herself "if I could just touch the hem of His garment I would be made whole." What a powerful decision she made in her desperation to be healed. And we all know the rest of the story. She was made whole. Jesus commended her faith. Just as she decided she received. What does this teach us? That God is not holding out on anyone of us. The decision is ours to make whether we desire to be healed or would rather relish in a condition of "woe is me" in order to attract the attention of others. May I say that the latter will result in utter misery.

The Holy Spirit has come to live inside us to teach us and to make all things clear to us. He is the Spirit of truth and is willing ready and able to lead us into the truth of our situation, even recalling things to our memories which could aid us to know hidden things and things not quite clear to our natural minds which when we act on His direction by faith we can be victorious! Perhaps your issue is not that of blood as illustrated in this woman's physical condition, but you are nevertheless bleeding in your memories and painful emotions of the past. There is no other place of restoration, healing and wholeness from emotional wounding than the cross of the Lord Jesus Christ. True life and new beginnings are found only at the cross.

A LITTLE FAMILY HISTORY

I am the last of seven children born to my mother. Three of these she bore prior to her marriage to my father. The last four [including me] after the said marriage. My father was a rather peculiar man, who rarely smiled, conversed, or appeared approachable. Nevertheless, he was an excellent provider for his family, and was driven by high expectations for us his four children. His relationship with us I would say was more or less based on academic achievements during our early years and young adulthood. Besides regular school attendance, he arranged for us to attend music lessons- [my two sisters and I played the piano] and my brother the violin]. We also went to ballet classes where my sisters and I were privileged to participate in several recitals and concert performances. We also received some private tutoring in after school programs.

My mother was a housewife, and really not a part of the planning of our lives when it came to school or extra curricular activities. Her role as I knew it was just cooking, washing and keeping the house. She was pretty active in community events and loved politics.

I was always very close to her [maybe as I was her last child] so she took me along to all of these community functions and I did have a lot of fun.

At home, sitting around the dining table at nights with home work books spread out, and having our father diligently inspect our school work done during the day was normal. His strict personality always made me somewhat afraid. He was the one who decided on our clothing, selecting the seamstress and taking us directly to her for our measurements and fittings. My mother was not involved in any of these things. Dental appointments and eye examinations were all arranged by him alone.

THE YEARS OF TURBULENCE

Our home during these years also became infused with several fights between my parents. There were times when my sisters and I would try to get involved in an effort to stop my father from physically hurting my mother because he became an alcoholic. After drinking sessions with his friends, he would come home and very often it took only a simple situation to begin a fight. As fighting and drinking continued, we all as children got involved. There was one particular day when my dad came home in such a badly drunken state and as the fighting started, my sisters and I got involved. He turned from my mother and began to chase after us. I paused to shout at him to leave my mother but he came after me instead with the fiercest countenance, shouting "you don't even know who your real father is". This statement went deep into my soul and became one of the deepest wounds of my heart. I was so very young and my life during those tender years became very, very confusing. I could not explain to any one what turmoil I was going through- because I did not understand it myself.

Besides this I encountered times of physical abuse from my father for no particular reason. I recall one night been beaten excessively over the spelling of one word. The word was part of a home work assignment and I had spelt it incorrectly. I had difficulty in concentrating and so to spell the word "disease" was a huge problem for me to commit to memory. My father delivered to me one agonizing blow after another with a large leather belt for each letter until I knew the spelling of that word. My mother stood by helplessly and was not able to rescue me.

Besides this, in attending my music lessons class, I was continually molested by my music lessons teacher, who was about 60 years old or more at the time. He always waited until there were no students around to approach me. I never said anything to my parents or to any one because I was so afraid and naïve. This man was like a father in seniority and so I could not understand why he continued to overwhelm me. It would seem that my heart was really searching for my father's love and I did not even know it. I was so very vulnerable that even when a 30 year old fellow music student asked me to come into his car, I went and he took me to a quiet place and sexually abused me. Here I was in my tender teen years and introduced to so many miseries of life. I did not realize that wounds were developing within me. So intense was the pain; the yearning for my father's love- for him to hug me, to correct me in love and to protect me. I felt like someone living in a house but still cast out into the open and very, very vulnerable. I struggled with the statement "you don't even know who your real father is". Then the question which plagued me was "who then is my real father"? It is obvious that my father's state of mind at the time he used this statement was under the control of alcohol, but how could a young child even begin to process this accurately? I really could not. This penetrated so very deep as a bruise would and lived quietly within me as everything else that took place in my life.

As my academic achievements dwindled my heart began to search for love. I became a person on the run searching hurting and searching in and out of relationships, while a very destructive sinful pattern was at work in my life.

MAN-GOD'S REPRESENTATIVE IN THE EARTH.

Families are extremely important to the heart of God. Satan knew and still knows this, so in order to destroy and corrupt man, he started in the Garden of Eden with the first family. Adam was given a command from God and was responsible for his wife and subsequently to demonstrate the Fatherhood of God to the children that were to be born to him and his wife Eve.

God the Father created men to be true fathers, husbands and protectors to their families: To love, shelter and to care for them. When this responsibility is abdicated, children can be left with a false and wrong concept of who God really is, and go through a life long struggle to accept Him as a Loving Father. The Bible emphatically says that "God is love". *1 John 4:16.*

I encourage fathers to be the first example of God's love that your children will ever know. Let them know the purity of a father's hug or compliment and really build a structure of godliness for your daughters and sons. I refer to the purity of a father's embrace, because we live in a time where satan continues to feverishly redefine the family and has succeeded in many ways to introduce to this generation aspects of "perverted love", emanating from ungodly lifestyles and many are being drawn into his wicked deception.

In spite of some of the negative things which happened during those early years, my father I believe did the best to provide for us and we were well provided for. Nevertheless there was always something deep within me that craved attention, love and a sense of belonging. I wandered around aimlessly at such an early age in relationships which could have destroyed me had it not been for the Hand of God. You see there is a place in each one of our lives which cannot be filled with things people or pleasures of sin, but is reserved for God alone. As parents no matter how good our intentions may be we have all the flaws of fallen humanity and if there is no experience of the new born life in Christ Jesus, there is not much that we could offer to our children to prepare them for a successful future filled with hope, peace and joy. Life truly begins with Jesus Christ and if a home has no foundation of the truth which is in Jesus Christ, dysfunction is the inevitable result for many. The truth is that we have all come from some type of dysfunction.

I was completely dysfunctional. After attempting a nursing career which was sponsored and encouraged by my father at the age of 17, I felt a sense of hope that something new was about to happen for me. Soon enough I gave birth to a daughter. My decision to leave my daughter with my parents so that I could at least complete this career did not help me very much to become stabilized, and I continued making several bad decisions resulting in colossal failures. I was not successful.

I embarked on a marriage relationship which ended no sooner than it began in a matter of months. By this time, my father became convinced that I needed to see a psychiatrist, and proceeded to send me to one. Just to interject a word of caution for those who use marriage as a means of escape from problems or a "cure for all" remedy for past hurts or failure- marriage cannot be used for a cover-up for pain, hurt or as a means of trying to find oneself. This could prove to be very devastating since marriage is a covenant established by our Heavenly Father. Neither of the two parties should enter into it for what they hope or expect to receive from each other in any impure way, but enter into it as an instrument of impartation. Not with motives of receiving in any given area of emotional need which you may have. Doing so can cause one party to make unreasonable demands upon the other expecting him or her to fulfill certain needs that only God can. This can happen particularly when there is a desperate need to be securely loved all the time. You see God never intended us to be fulfilled by each other but by Him alone. Our spousal relationships are an extension of Who He is in our individual lives, and should be the vehicle through which we help and minister to each other. He is the only One who can make us whole and love us unconditionally and perfectly. At those early stages of my life, I never knew this. I had no knowledge of God as regards to His love, grace or provision of salvation. My life was totally surrounded by pain, insecurity and I definitely developed a very low self esteem.

DEEP NEED

I saw no way out of what was happening to me, but my inner problems and emotional conflicts grew in intensity. I was extremely needy, searching for love and validation, significance and a way to feel happy and secure. There were times that I would take my father's money, not because I personally needed anything for myself, but I did it to buy friends. I searched for significance, and the need for someone to at least like me. I did not even like myself, and felt so much alienation and rejection from the people whom I really wanted to care for me that I sought ways to find someone who could say something positive about me. I guess my father's way of helping was to assign me to a psychiatrist who admitted me to the psychiatric unit. Strong medications were pumped into me which caused me to suffer many side effects. There was also a decision to carry out shock treatment which was not administered, thank God. I was so emotionally bankrupt, weak and blinded by pain that even though I was already an adult I never objected to any of the decisions my father made for me at the time. I just went right along. Even when spiritists [people who were obviously from the occultic world were brought to our home by my father who claimed that they were there to assist in my healing I just went right along with whatever was brought to me. One of them was from a place call Java. She said that I needed to lose some weight so she set up a series of steam baths and also brought pebbles or stones to me asking me to put my thoughts into them. The equipment for the steam baths was placed in the living room of our home and I never questioned my father's decisions. None of my siblings were subject to any of these things and I seem to be singled out. My mother was silent and quietly or maybe fearfully went along without objection. I believe that she truly loved me but had no power in herself to help me. She faithfully visited me while I was in the psychiatric unit, brought me meals and continued to show me the care and concern of a good mother. She also had a dear friend who was like a mother to me and who also visited me all the time and comforted me. On my release from the hospital I stayed at the home of this dear woman until I was strong enough.

As time went by so quickly I faced rejection and fear and also became rebellious and bitter. The daughter I gave birth to was raised by my parents and her heart was turned against me. I began to sense a great alienation and distance between my father and I and this obviously affected my relationship with my daughter. She was told many negative things about me and all the plans concerning her life were handed over to my sisters' control. I felt like a complete outcast and as though I did not even exist. I grew very fearful of my father, but mixed with that negative emotion was rebellion. No one knew my inner pain, or silent suffering, nor could I explain it to any one. No one would have believed and so all of my actions and reactions were continually misunderstood. The more I craved my father's love and acceptance, the more he turned away from me. My siblings were not very bonded with me either so I was always very much alone. Apart from my mother's companionship most of the time I felt very alienated. Even in family gatherings I still felt alone, secluded and shut out for some reason, while my daughter's rejection and eventual rebellion against me led to arguments with my parents and much strife. This became a severe wound in my heart. As I continued down this very dark path, relationships became my temporary ease for the intense pain, loneliness and confusion which I felt. My father wanted me to have nothing to do with my daughter! This was unbelievable. There were times that I could not even go into the house when he was there, for my mother would give me a sign that he was there and I dared not go in. This produced much fear in me.

As questions continued in my mind without answers, I recalled when I first returned from London after my failed nursing career, my mother shared with me about my father's involvement in activities within an organization, which even though I did not know anything about satan's devices, I knew that it was evil. He kept evil books in his book cabinet and never shared a room or bed with my mother. He prayed with certain candles in the darkness using a mirror to look into and my mother and I came to the full conclusion that he was drawn into some thing evil. There was no knowledge of the saving grace of Jesus Christ and being born again throughout my entire family from as far back as I could remember and have experienced. I grew up and knew the Catholic faith from my childhood until the Lord saved me by His grace at the age of thirty-two...

Relief for my pain was nowhere in sight for me before this neither could I tell anyone what I was experiencing so I suffered silently. Having lost my job and career, I was in a terrible shape and everyone thought that I was truly out of my mind. Nothing was further from the truth. I needed to find myself, I needed God and in my search I embarked upon some perilous pathways.

pamela b h victor

As I look back now, I know that the hand and mercy of God were upon me even then.

With two other children born to me [another daughter and a son], my deep desire which is the heart of any mother was to have all my children grow together; so I pursued ways to reunite my oldest daughter with her siblings, so we could all be together. Each time my efforts were futile. I was continually coming up to an insurmountable wall and an upheaval would occur between my parents and I. It left unpleasant memories and I just could not understand my father's reason for hating me in this way even to the point of taking away my own child. Now I do realize that he was controlled by the powers of darkness due to his involvement in certain occult practices. As feelings of loneliness drove me to seek solace in relationships, I became even more insecure in every way. Accompanied by feelings of rejection by family members, and no real sociable atmosphere of friends, I just roamed through life in an aimless fashion looking for love and acceptance, I did not realize then that the emotional afflictions of my childhood were leading me down a path of destruction due to sinful responses on my part.

SEARCHING FOR CURES: NEGATIVE RESPONSES AND REACTIONS CAN BE VERY DESTRUCTIVE.

Verbal and physical abuse, sorrow grief and affliction may come in various forms as these are launched viciously against our lives in a fallen world through fallen humanity in need of God.

If our responses to these evils are fed by anger, resentment, bitterness, and unforgiveness, we will be led into pathways of sin and destruction. Failure to deal with pain and hurt and refusal to acknowledge what is going on in our emotional system causes us to block out what should be dealt with openly. It also opens the door for the father of lies [satan] to enter in to deceive us.

Many times we do not know how to deal with what has happened to us throughout life and it becomes a secret – buried deep beneath layers and layers of pain. In most cases the trauma was not our fault, but we are afraid to come out onto the open lest we be censored and judged by people who do not understand. This puts us in a position to continue to remain silent while we suffer and search for answers in all the wrong places.

Here is where satan comes in to introduce what I call "narcotics" bringing a temporary relief and giving a "false high" or fix to numb the pain, pushing it deeper and deeper into our hearts where roots become established and dependency is the result. These "narcotics" may take the form of sex, money, position, success, validation, or activity – the workaholic mentality. You see there is a need to feel secure, loved and validated wherever there is shame from the past. Relationships serve as a "cover" up" or "cure" and are usually filled with jealousy, control, and manipulation. Since we do not want to lose out or be hurt and rejected all over again, we try to keep relationships centered on our personal need and not on the need of others. Seeking cures for pain which was buried deep within me, and my lack of understanding of how to deal with it pushed me more and more towards relationships. These were always short lived because I was searching for the healing and wholeness while wounds became deeper. The pain would ease for a while, only to begin all over again when the relationship ended. Rejection was what I experienced time and again, as relationships started and ended abruptly. My first marriage was one of those which ended in separation and eventually divorce. This could have been termed as an annulment since it really only lasted for a few months.

With a low self esteem and feelings of no self worth it is very easy to become "everybody's everything" so to speak. Since what you look for is genuine love and acceptance, in an unhealed emotional dilemma, relationships pose as the answer to the problem, but are really satan's big deceptive plot. Until a genuine encounter with the Agape love of God is experienced, there can be no healing or wholeness. You see when your belief system is wrong and confused you think that sex makes you feel loved. It actually boils down to a very low pattern of demoralized self esteem where you feel you are of no worth or of little value in life. If all through your life you've thought that relationships can make you feel significant then you must realize that significance does not come from this source. Only Christ Jesus can give our lives any sense of worth or value. We were created by God and if he thought that we were of no value He would not send His precious Son to die for us to redeem us back to Himself. "You made all the delicate inner parts of my body and knit me together in my mother's womb. You watched me as I was being formed in utter seclusion, as I was woven together in the dark of the womb. You saw me before I was born. Every day of my life was recorded in your book. Every moment was laid out before a single day had passed." *Psalm 139:13,15,16. NLT. NEW LIVING TRANSLATION.* We have been fearfully and wonderfully made.

Plunging into a relationship with someone twenty six years my senior gave me some temporary relief. I felt somewhat secure and good about myself because he became like a father who showed care and provided well. I was esteemed [or so it appeared to be] and it seemed like the ideal situation. He helped me in many ways and a ray of "hope" began to beam forth for me. I thought to myself that I would not be hurt again. It did not take very long before all my problems resurfaced. My two children were not very happy and my first daughter was alienated more and more and I continued to remain in a perpetual state of pain. It would seem that my first child had developed wounds of her own and hatred towards me as she continued to hear negative reports about me. Even though I lived on the top floor of my parents' home, my father refused to have anything to say to me. My mother intervened for me to be there at that time since I had nowhere to go. I lived in constant fear and could not venture to the floor where he lived whenever he was at home. As I searched desperately within myself for answers regarding his rejection of me, I was literally tormented. There were times when I would lie down to sleep and have nightmare after nightmare of him chasing me, running after me; and I would be running away from him so he would not hurt me. My mother offered no explanation and I became so emotionally devastated that I felt I could not go on. He would have my sisters buy me gifts for birthdays or for Christmas [something he did for each of us] but he maintained his stand-off position towards me.

CONVERSION EXPERIENCE

I want to take this opportunity to recall my born again experience before going through the stages which the Lord used to lead me to healing and victory.

As I continued in the relationship with the man who was twenty six years my senior, we shared the apartment in my parents' home together. For the first time in my life I began to feel very uneasy about my life and my mind tossed back and forth concerning a decision to partake in a festival of revelry which we always took part in. [This uneasiness I found out afterwards as being the convicting power of the Holy Spirit]. I of course did not know this at the time. As I went to my kitchen I heard a distinct voice say these words : "Choose you this day whom you shall serve." I was frightened and looked around to see who was there. No one was in the house but me and my companion. He did not hear anything. This made me panic but I did not say anything. The next day as I went to my place of employment I approached a young girl who I knew to be a Christian and told her my experience. She opened her bible and showed the scripture to me. She told me that I had to make the choice to serve the Lord, but she did not lead me to Him right away. It was like God began to do a quick work, because my two children were invited to a nearby Pentecostal Church where the Sunday school workers came to transport them to church on Sundays. The first day that I visited this church, which was two weeks after my experience with this voice, I met with the Pastor and his wife after the service and told them what I had experienced. They both confirmed that the Lord w as calling me.

At the invitation of someone in my neighborhood to a tent crusade I responded on the first night of the meeting to an altar call to receive Jesus into my heart and to be forgiven of my sins. I ran down the aisle and fell on my knees, weeping uncontrollable over my sins. A counselor was praying for me and all I could feel was such a peace coming upon my life. When I got up from that place I knew that something different had happened to me. I walked away knowing that I was wonderfully saved and that Jesus had come into my heart and cleansed me of my sins. It was such a beautiful and clean feeling!

The dilemma that I immediately faced concerning my companion was how to discontinue this relationship. He too had come down to the altar, but I doubted whether he had the same conversion experience as I did, and had reasons for feeling this way. Nevertheless we both attended a class for new Christians at the same little church my children attended. We got married and were baptized in water. This marriage lasted for seven years and then ended in separation.

SERVING WITH CONTINUED BONDAGE

As I continued to attend church and fellowship with other Christians, I was enjoying my new life in Christ and soon was asked to lead a women's group and serve in other areas. I was willing to be available where needed even though I did not have much experience. Being active, I believe was one way to keep me from having to face some of the turmoil which was still going on in my life of which I could tell no one. I was battling with emotional bondage and scars which I never realized were so deep until the Lord made me aware of what was going on in my heart. This was for the express purpose of healing me and leading me to wholeness.

The church I attended though legalistic in the teaching and principles, offered me a strong stable foundation in Christ and there was a profound bond of God's love and fellowship and caring in the congregation. Even with this atmosphere in the church, I began to experience attacks of guilt and condemnation from time to time. I developed a wrong concept of God, and because of all the wounds of the past, whenever negative situations would arise I thought that God was punishing me. I heard a lot of preaching about hell and punishment and even though I knew that I was no longer going there, I fell into a cycle of trying to please God so He would accept me; just as I was trying to get my earthly father to accept me, and to love me. The more I tried the more I failed. I experienced many hardships and difficulties and each time I bought the lie of the devil who said that God did not love me and was punishing me for my past. I fasted, prayed read my bible trying to find some relief and to be acceptable to God, while continuing to repent over the same things again and again.

ON THE ROAD TO HEALING

What I discovered was that I was reliving my past continually and did not know how to get beyond the wall of condemnation which I continued to run into. In God's divine timing and purpose, He led me to a church where the grace and mercy of God was preached with much clarity. God sat me down and began to do a deep work in my life. This happened eleven years after I was saved. Various trips to the altar in response to the Word of God brought tremendous healing and deliverance to me. God spoke directly to my pain, to my past, to my rejection and trauma. He used His servants to teach me about His great mercy and grace. I became so broken as God pulled out the pain by the roots. Unforgiveness was binding me because of all the wrongs which I felt were done to me, and condemnation for the wrongs I did in my past. I nursed and rehearsed the past and blamed people for being responsible for my condition, instead of taking responsibility for my own actions which we all must do. I had relished on the past to such an extent that I could not see anything good coming forth for my future – only negativity. I could not see myself as a new creature in Christ Jesus or the righteousness of God in Him.

Even though I knew the Word of God and could quote the scriptures, there was no good fruit in my life for God because I kept reliving my past. I was so wounded that there were scars which only the Holy Spirit could see and heal as a sovereign work of grace. It was as though a light suddenly went on and I saw myself and my whole life before me and then began to understand as the Lord showed me my wounded heart.

EMOTIONAL WOUNDING.

ISAIAH 53:4-5
Surely He has borne our grief and carried our sorrows and pains of punishment, yet we ignorantly considered Him stricken, smitten and afflicted by God. But He was wounded for our transgressions, he was bruised for our guilt and iniquities, the chastisement needed to obtain peace and well being for us was upon Him, and with the stripes that wounded Him we are healed and made whole."

Now when it comes to emotional wounding and the healing of our emotions, we must understand that our emotions are a vital part of our make up. Herein resides our feelings, sensitivities, passions, thought, reasoning, desires and much more. They react to pain and pressure and can affect our destiny for good or for bad. What we have heard, seen felt or experienced can affect our decisions, actions and our character. God does not intend for us to rely on our emotions for guidance through life because very often they can be very deceiving due to the fallen nature of our souls. What compounds the wounding of our emotions are the negative and sinful responses which we give in to. All such responses lead to bitterness, unforgiveness, strife and revenge. If you are a child of God and you feel victimized due to your past, which has left you so torn that no matter how hard you try to serve the Lord you lack that fullness of joy which He has provided for you, you may need to consider a few things. Have you truly faced up to the challenge of those circumstances no matter how painful they have been, and brought them to God so that the power of His grace can be released into your life to heal your wounded heart? Only He can do this by the power of His Holy Spirit, but He awaits your corporation! Remember that the Holy Spirit is a Helper, not an overtaker; what does a Helper do? He helps you in your willingness to allow Him to enter into your circumstances and takes hold as it were with your mutual participation as He works alongside you. As He guides us through this healing process He may lead through His Word directly or through a human vessel or a variety of other means which He may choose. His purpose is to assist us in finding the root issues to our problems, so we can have victory. No matter what has taken place in our lives we are also accountable and responsible before God for the way we respond in any given situation. We must therefore own up and take responsibility for our actions and reactions to what was done to us. How about forgiveness? Maybe you may say "never! I may forgive but not forget; how can I ever forgive them?" Well Jesus taught us over and over again that forgiveness is mandatory to real victory. There can be no long term healing as long as we remain in an attitude of bitterness and hold on to buried grudges towards a person or persons involved. If you really desire to be healed, then receiving God's grace of forgiveness and forgiving the wrong doer must be understood. These are twin ingredients which must be worked into every situation in order to bring forth fruitful victorious living. If you have stumbled over the foundational truth of God's love for you, and it has not become a living reality and a revelation, you must ask the Holy Spirit to help you and give you the grace to understand how much He really loves you, and the true meaning of His forgiveness towards you. Always remember that the person who wronged you can never do anything to fully pay you back in a manner that fully satisfies you for what was done. Forgiveness is a gift given to the undeserved. None of us deserved it or ever will. Jesus paid every sin debt in full, so to demand mentally a payment from another person is truly wrong for any of us to do. Jesus did not deserve to die a criminal's death; we deserved it altogether. He gave His life a ransom for many, so that we might be freed from the terror and penalty of sin and it's consequences and be forgiven. When we were yet sinners Christ died for us. If we hold on to the pain of the past and fail to forgive, we continue to be emotionally hooked to the person, persons or circumstances involved and the wounds in our emotions will not be healed. We must be willing to release people from this emotional hook and so allow God to work both in our lives and also in their lives. I am convinced that emotional wounding is so much worst than physical wounding, because in the physical realm, everyone can quickly see what has happened to you and even offer you some professional help or advice in the best way they can. Medical doctors can do great things to relieve physical wounds and bring about some form of healing but no one can reach into the depths of the human soul to truly effect the healing on the emotions. Only Jesus can do this since only His eyes can penetrate and see the damage and brokenness of a soul. Emotional wounding can go deep into a person's heart and remains there producing constant pain. It comes like someone stabbed you in the chest or back and left the knife there. The words and actions of others can be like drawn swords. [Psalms 55:21]. They pierce deeply and go into the memories of the afflicted one. With hurt memories you could hardly function normally. Too much has happened, you saw too much, experienced too much and the pain of the past continues with you driving you to seek for answers and a place of rest and closure from these unpleasant issues.

I have experienced bruising and have seen people bruised physically from a fall or from a blow inflicted on them or some other injury. It first turns black and blue and is extremely painful. It also takes a long time to heal and to clear up. The effect of this type of injury goes deep into the levels of the skin and tissue. Touching the affected area in the natural triggers great pain; likewise if our emotions are bruised and wounded, when the issues are touched or brought to memory, pain results. According to the intensity and longevity of the circumstances, which caused the wounds, there is a release of poisons; so nothing filters out but bitterness, grief and hate. When you think of the issues you cry and agonize and wish they never happened or wonder why they ever did. I cried time and time again, and could come up with no answers. I saw myself as a victim until the Lord freed me. He heals the memories and removes the venomous poison and malignancy of the emotional cancer rendering it ineffective to do us any more harm.

This is what the Lord did for me; the fruit that results from His healing power can be nothing but love, joy, and peace and all that His Presence produces. You see Jesus, according to *Isaiah 53 4-5*, bore our grief, sorrows and sickness; was wounded for our transgressions and bruised for our iniquities. It means that the wounds He received was for those who transgressed against us and for the transgressions and iniquities which we were born with through Adam's sin, those we commit through our span of life, and those we committed when we reacted in sinful ways to cover up our pain and shame as well as future mistakes and sins. Abuse cannot be healed except by the precious blood of Jesus Christ, which has healing restoring power. Any other form of false covering will produce negative effects, because pain buried within will find a way to express itself out. Rejection as I understand it is one of the greatest forms of emotional abuse because it comes most times from sources close to us in some measure and from people that we tend to look up to or have made ourselves vulnerable to at some point in our lives. Also when you have such a need that you want to fit in with a certain group or person and they end up treating you with slant courtesy this could also open up a door for rejection to begin to nest itself in a person's life. There is also parental rejection and rejection from the womb which can transfer itself in some way to an infant child and can be the beginning stages of a lifetime of pain and confusion. We were made to be loved and when we lack the knowledge of God's love for us or are doubtful of it in any way we would seek that love in other illegitimate ways which eventually lead to pain and brokenheartedness.

Before the Lord began dealing with me and beginning this deep work in my emotions by His grace, I was a captive. I knew that I was on my way to heaven to escape hell and this was good news for me but how to live here on earth and have victory in knowing that I am a child of God and that He is not condemning me for my past was unknown to me. I pictured God as the person who was waiting for me to make a mistake and then punish me for it.

I felt like He was hiding His face from me and not willing to help me. Due to this deception I felt hopeless thinking that nothing I ever did pleased Him. This picture was of course the image in my mind of a "god" who did these things because this was all that I had known. It was not the truth about the True and Living God Who loved me enough to send His only begotten Son to this earth to die for me so that I could have a changed life and walk in fellowship with Him and live for eternity with Him because He loved me so very much. Growing up in an environment where the love grace, and mercy of God is not known can make one think that everything you do wrong or every mistake you make "God's going to get you for that". I knew and have heard words like "God will punish you"; not necessarily only referring to me but to anyone else who may have done something wrong. This was the "god" that most people knew at that time; a "god" who was busy throwing out retribution on humanity continually. The exact opposite is true of The True and Living God who created the heavens and the earth and all that there is , who sent His Son to die for the human race so He could bring us back into fellowship with Him. If this were not at all so then no one could ever be able to approach Him, know Him or be able to come to Him; more than that we would never be able to share His home with Him in heaven when life on earth is over. His nature is love, and if we would check out His character throughout the Bible we would discover that He is always doing everything He can to call mankind to Himself. He desires to love and forgive and make His plan known to people so that He could do them good. He has a good plan for each person and is willing to reveal it as we submit to Him and follow what He said. Negative emotions like anger, wrath and bitterness and even vengeance due to emotional pain caused by a traumatic situation or unjust act can trigger people who have been victimized to wish or desire the worst to come on the perpetrator. If the act of the wrong doer is punishable by the law the person will be dealt with accordingly. If they would turn to the Lord and accept His offer of forgiveness and mercy, though they still have to face consequences for doing evil, God's mercy and grace flows to them and He will give them His peace as they acknowledge their sin before Him. A clear example of this was fully demonstrated on Calvary where two thieves were being crucified with Jesus. One railed at Him in arrogance and pride saying "if thou be Christ save thyself and us". The other humbled himself and rebuked him saying "dost not thou fear God seeing thou art in the same condemnation? And we indeed justly ; for we receive the due reward for our deeds: but this man has done nothing amiss." *Luke 29 23:39-43 King James Bible* The repentant thief immediately asked the Lord to remember him when He came into His kingdom and the request was granted but the deserved punishment was carried through.

God's ways are not our ways and He does whatever He pleases. The Apostle Paul formerly called Saul gives an account of himself and his former sinful actions as an injurious person and a blasphemer, one who wasted the church and persecuted Christians hauling them to prison and beating them while consenting to their deaths; He said "but I obtained mercy , because I did it ignorantly in unbelief. And the grace of God was exceeding abundant with faith and love which is in Christ Jesus" *1 Timothy 1:12-14 King James Bible* He called himself the chief of all sinners.

Pain is legitimate in all such circumstances to those who have been wronged, but can be compounded by these negative emotions which when one functions in that realm for a long time it can begin to take a toll even on their physical well being. We must remember that no amount of anger or hoping the worst thing to happen to the wrong doer or parties concerned, would ever help wounded people to heal or be restored; the damage in most cases may be irreparable and irreplaceable, so leaving situations to a just God and not trying to be in His place gives Him an opportunity to move in and do what He knows is right. Remember that His nature is love and mercy and though we may not be able to understand this due to blinding pain it is wise for our own good to release people to God. He is always right. Meanwhile if people continue to operate in the realm of negative emotions this in and of itself is sin. He never leaves judgement or vengeance up to us as individuals because He knows we will always handle it the wrong way due to our emotional make up. He is no respecter of persons and will deal with everyone as He sees fit. Also it is good for us to know that mercy withholds from people what we really deserve and grace gives to us what we do not deserve. This is what the sacrifice of Jesus on the cross means to all of us, and as long as we embrace this truth we will surely realize that none of us deserve to be forgiven but to be punished; but because of His great love for us all God put Jesus in our place so that we do not have to pay personally the penalty for sin, for as the bible says all have sinned and come short of the glory of God. He never desires the death or destruction of a sinner or wrong doer, but rather that the person repents and turns to Him for forgiveness; [death here does not merely imply physical death but that which is eternal separation from God]. His delight is to show mercy and because of this His mercies are new every morning. If they were not many of us would not be even here today! People can choose their own destinies because God is not a dictator; He offers life and a chance for everyone to change and be forgiven and have peace. He will by no means clear the guilty; Exodus 34:7. Those who by their own wills refuse to accept His offer of forgiveness and mercy remain in their sins and transgressions and will affect their own eternal destinies negatively. God does not make light of heartbreaking situations which plunge people into grief and despair. He is a just God. He cares enough to offer divine solutions that will ease the suffering and reveal His love so we could trust Him. You do not have to interact with the one who has wronged or abused you whether it is a parent, spouse, stranger, child or other, but your response toward God concerning each situation must be forgiveness. Reconciliation is most times on another level which God's grace can take us through especially in family relationships or acquaintances. I also want to point out to anyone reading this book that if you do not know Jesus Christ as you Lord and Saviour, you will not be able to easily release someone who has harmed you or those concerning you naturally. You need the help of the Holy Spirit to live within you to give you the strength and grace to do so. God does not expect you to do this in your own strength. I have included a prayer at the end of this book so that you may accept His offer of mercy and receive Jesus as your Lord and Saviour; this is the first step but not the final one on your journey towards healing, restoration and wholeness.

Romans 5:1-6. AMP. Amplified Bible
"Therefore, since we are justified [acquitted, declared righteous, and given a right standing with God] through faith, let us [grasp the fact that we] have [the peace of reconciliation to hold and to enjoy] peace with God through our Lord Jesus Christ [the Messiah, the Anointed One]. Through him also we have [our] access [entrance, introduction] by faith into this grace [state of God's favor in which we [firmly and safely] stand. And let us rejoice and exult in our hope of experiencing and enjoying the glory of God. Moreover [let us also be full of joy now!] let us exult and triumph in our troubles and rejoice in our sufferings, knowing that pressure and affliction and hardship produce patient and unswerving endurance. And endurance [fortitude] develops maturity of character [approved faith and tried integrity] and character [of this sort] produces [the habit of] joyful and confident hope of eternal salvation. Such hope never disappoints or deludes or shames us, for God's love has been poured out in our hearts through the Holy Spirit Who has been given to us. While we were yet in weakness [powerless to help ourselves] at the fitting time Christ died for [on behalf of] the ungodly." Romans 5:8-9. AMP.Amplified Bible.

33

"But God shows and clearly proves His own love for us by the fact that while we were still sinners [Christ the Messiah, the Anointed One] died for us. Therefore since we are now justified [acquitted, made righteous, and brought into right relationship with God] shall be saved by Him from the indignation and wrath of God."
Romans 5:15-16. AMP. Amplified Bible.

"But God's free gift is not at all to be compared to the trespass [His grace is out of proportion to the fall of man]. For if many died through one man's falling away [his lapse, his offense], much more profusely did God's grace and the free gift [that comes] through the undeserved favor of the one Man, Jesus Christ abound and overflow to and for [the benefit] of many. Nor is the free gift at all to be compared to the effort of that [man's] sin. For the sentence [following the trespass] of one [man] brought condemnation, whereas the free gift [following] many transgressions brings justification [an act of righteousness]."

The above verses have been of tremendous help to me and continue to be because the Holy Spirit [my Helper, Counselor and Comforter] *John 14:26 AMP.* has made, and continues to make these very clear to my inner man.

Jesus told His disciples [and this includes every born again believer] "I have told you these things while I am still with you, but the Comforter[Counselor, Helper, Intercessor, Advocate, Strengthener, Standby], the Holy Spirit, Whom the Father will send in My Name [in My place to represent Me and act on My behalf] He will teach you all things. And cause you to recall [will remind you or bring to your remembrance] everything I have told you." *John 14:26. AMP Amplified Bible.*

RECEIVING THE LOVE OF GOD.

We must believe and put our faith in God's love for us or we will be like leaves tossed in the wind, never learning to rest in His wonderful provision. This is very important to emotionally abused or wounded people who have been hurt by authority figures or others and are afraid to approach Him.

The key for us is to recognize that He is merciful and gracious and kind, otherwise it is easy to develop the kind of fear towards Him which results in dread, rather than drawing near to Him in reverential fear and with the understanding that He is a loving Father. *Romans 5:2* says that we have an entrance, or introduction by faith into this grace [state of God's favor] in which we [firmly and safely] stand. *Amplified Bible.* We are safe when we go to God because Jesus our Great High Priest is at the Father's right hand interceding for us. *Hebrews 4:14-16.*

This has nothing to do with trying to please God. He has already accepted us. This cannot be changed even when we make a mistake or sin. When we run to the precious blood of Jesus for immediate cleansing and renewal through repentance, that sin will not have dominion over us. I really want to get this point through as the Holy Spirit helps me because so many people are trying to please God by good works, particularly those who suffer from some form of low self-esteem or have come from abusive backgrounds; there are others who are legalistic and want to be recognized by their good works.

We cannot establish our own righteousness. God has already done this through Christ's death and resurrection and our making Him Lord of our lives. We cannot try to please God in ourselves, or make ourselves acceptable to Him. We are the "called" and the "chosen" to the praise of His glorious grace. *Ephesians 2:6.* The Holy Spirit helps us in our walk with the Lord so that we can please Him. He continues to woo us and speak to us in many ways so that we would be more like Jesus. This is His ultimate goal. Our duty is to yield to Him every time. The good news is that our sins are forgiven, our consciences can be cleansed from guilt and made pure and we can approach

God without fear and fellowship with Him through His Holy Spirit; there Jesus presents our prayers and petitions to our loving Heavenly Father.

THE IMAGE OF CHRIST: GOING FROM GLORY TO GLORY

Man was created in the image of God and even though the devil moved in to darken that image through Adam's fall, God sent Jesus to restore His image in us by reconciling us to Himself.

The manifestation is from within us. The Holy Spirit is constantly at work in our lives desiring to change us, but He does need our cooperation. God's plan of salvation is the restoration of the total man--- spirit, soul and body. Our spirits are redeemed when we make Jesus the Lord of our lives as a sovereign work of grace done by the Holy Spirit. Our souls- made up of our minds, wills and emotions will continue to undergo the constant progressive work of the Holy Spirit Who lives in us and continues to draw us to partake of more of the life of Jesus, so that we live spirit filled spirit led lives. It's that process of sanctification and consecration. Our bodies will eventually be changed into a new and glorified state at the return of our blessed Lord. The purpose of the Holy Spirit is to change us from glory to glory until that final day, and He does this by restoring our souls and transforming us into the image of Christ through renewing our minds with the word of God.

There will always be lingering struggles which we will all have to face from time to time as we move up in God. There are levels of growth and discipline and heights and depths which we are yet to discover, so that we can never reach to a point in our Christian walk that we can say "I've arrived". Anytime that we reach to a place like this where we feel we have already achieved what we need in life or are not prepared to learn more about Jesus, we make ourselves of no use to the Great Potter. He is still making vessels of clay....shaping and reshaping. We are His workmanship recreated in Christ Jesus that we might do the good works which He called us to do. *Ephesians 2:10.*

I have been through stages in my own life when God had to interrupt my schedule in His dealings with me when I drifted back into unbelief or looking to the arm of flesh, while entertaining doubt and fear about my circumstances. There were times of definite lessons and teachings of the Holy Spirit which helped me not to forget the mercy and the Fatherhood of God, which I found myself doing while slipping into self-pity and thinking of Him the wrong way all over again.

When He brings the searchlight of the Holy Spirit to beam on such areas, our response should always be that of humbling ourselves before Him in prayer, so that He can reveal Himself to us afresh as being high and lifted up. Then our only response would be to worship Him because of Who He is.

There is a tremendous difference between Praise and Worship. We can praise God for a number of things and His many benefits which He freely bestows on us and we must. We should praise Him in thankfulness for our homes, our jobs, health, families, safety, and so many things which He gives to us. Worship is on a higher level, in so much that we should be able to say "God I worship you just because of Who you are; even though I don't know why some of these adversities are coming my way and I just can't seem to find a way out... none of these things make you less God; You will always be God and I worship You!" Our worship should be always centered on who God is and not on our particular need. We cannot continue to see Him through the eyes of our circumstances while we fuss and complain, rather than exalting Him so that He can take care of our needs according to His riches in glory by Christ Jesus.

GROWING IN GRACE

Sometimes problems can appear to be like great giants. You read the Word of God, and pray but you still doubt because the word is not mixed with faith. There were several times in my life when I have felt stuck in this particular realm and I 'm sure we all have. I loved God and knew that I was saved, but somehow was unable to go forward; I always reverted backwards to my past. The past was like a Jericho wall to me filled with wounds and memories. Before my healing I would hear preachers say "draw a line on your past"... But that was not so very simple to do.

When you are not yet in the healing school of the Holy Spirit you cannot just forget the past and move on. Only by the help of the Greater One inside of me could I have yielded to Him so He could do the work in my life. I had to also make a choice to trust God completely. This was God's time to help me and it was one step at time.

When God brought the children of Israel out of Egyptian bondage he promised them..."I will send the hornet before you....which shall drive out the Hivite the Cananite, and the Hittite from before thee. I will not drive them from before thee in one year, lest the land become desolate and the beast of the field multiply against thee" *Exodus 23:28-29. King James.* God wants us to possess our possessions and spiritual inheritance, but He takes us through the process in stages as we cooperate with Him. He will not force us. There is no way that we can go around situations. The counsel of the Lord stands sure. *Psalms 33:11.* The way to receive His counsel is by taking heed to the Word of God and meditating on it so that we may see ourselves as God sees us. If we are not anchored in God's Word then we will like the children of Israel retreat to the wilderness, because discouragement and fear are very real tools of the devil. When situations are not resolved in the time in which we would like them to be resolved and victory seems no where in sight, without a fresh look at God's ways as revealed through His Word, we will get to looking at the "giants" and become faint hearted. When doubts and discouragement fill our minds we must do what the psalmist said in *Psalms 94:18-19.* "I cried out, "I am slipping!" And your unfailing love, O Lord, supported me. When doubts filled my mind, your comfort gave me renewed hope and cheer." *NLT. New Living Translation.* We receive strength to go on and courage to press our way all the way to victory. We must go through, knowing that we are not alone. As we grow up, we will be prepared to put away childish things in exchange for more of Jesus and His resurrection life. God never forces us. He sets before us each day the opportunity to obey or disobey; He instructs us what we should do in order for us to have peace and joy but we can eventually choose our own path. His way is always right for He sets before us life and death, blessing and cursing, but instructs us to choose life for our own good and that of our descendants. Obedience leads us to eat the good fruit of the land while disobedience leads to reaping bitter fruit. Thank God that in His mercy He many times does not allow us to taste the full consequences of our own desires and self will, all of which I call the valley of experiences, but and if we do, this by no means indicates that He does not love us or care for us; but in the valley we do not have much choice but to trust Him and reach out for Him so that we can be lifted up to higher ground to be the blessing that He desires us to be. All of His dealings are out of His great love and care for us and He never leaves us. Remember that He is the God of the valley as well as the God who reigns on Mount Zion. As long as He leads us into the valley, there He will sustain and support us. He does whatever is necessary at the moment in order to move us on and into what He has called us to and to move us in closer to Himself. It's all about attaining the divine destiny and calling to which He has so called us. The end result will always be what He set out to accomplish in us, which is to see Jesus revealed in our lives more and more for His glory. We should crave the pure spiritual milk of the word of God as new born babies do and as we do this He will move us into receiving the strong meat which He intends for us to have when we are progressing in spiritual growth.

DEAD ISSUES

Some of the dead issues we carry stem from offenses of past pain and trauma. These can cause people to carry burdens which God never intended them to carry and they bring with them a certain stench......the stench of death. These issues can cause our lives to be defiled to a certain point, hence the reason God wants us to be totally sanctified; "and the very God of peace sanctify you wholly; and I pray God your whole spirit and soul and body be preserved blameless unto the coming of our Lord Jesus Christ. Faithful is He that calleth you who also will do it. *1 Thessalonians 5:23-24.* Remember that the bible says the law of the Spirit of life in Christ Jesus sets us free from the law of sin and death. Taking offense and bearing grudges and unforgiveness, are all companions of the law of sin and death and produce fruit unto death. The Holy Spirit longs to lead us into a life of forgiveness and wholeness. When we listen to the voice of the flesh we prolong our deliverance and allow the pain and hurt to remain in our lives. The Lord wants to make us whole so we can be vessels who demonstrate His resurrection life and healing saving power to this dying world. If we continue to choose to walk in the "death realm" as it were how can we lead this world to Jesus and His forgiving love and mercy? We have to first experience His love and mercy in a most powerful measure and live in it day by day allowing the Spirit of God to flow through us to this world. It is not enough to know certain biblical truths from a point of sense knowledge or head knowledge. God wants us to experience what He has laid down for us in His Word in such a way that we walk in it every day of our lives. If not we could be like the children of Israel with a veil on our minds and hearts and never experience what the Holy Spirit was sent into our lives to do.... That is to reveal Jesus in and through us, shaping us into Christ likeness. Remember that dead issues will imprison us, and hinder the work of the Holy Spirit, therefore let us humble ourselves before Him so that we can experience all that He has for us.

PURIFYING OUR HEARTS

We must be vigilant with what enters our hearts and minds for this is where strongholds are formed and thought patterns build up. It is where satan has his greatest plan of attack. He knows that this inner sanctuary is most precious to God and can be so easily polluted. What we allow to stay in our hearts will eventually be manifested in the way we behave. It will also affect our conversation, for out of the abundance of the heart the mouth speaks. We should never cover or protect any areas of character flaws but allow the sanctifying work of the Holy Spirit to produce within us the character of Christ more and more.

We are to renew our minds with the word of God and not be conformed to this world. *Romans 12:2.* Our hearts are most subtle and there are thoughts and attitudes which can settle there unknown to us. *Jeremiah 17:9.* God searches our hearts and tries the reins because He knows the battle which the enemy tries to engage us in, in an effort to defeat us in this vulnerable part of our beings. Knowing that the manifestation is from within we must do as the Apostle Paul admonished us and that is to cast down all high imaginations and every high thing which sets itself against the true knowledge of God.

It is written "Christ in you the hope of glory". *Colossians 1:27.* This is the manifestation that God has planned for us. David cries out in *Psalms 103:1.* "Bless the Lord O my soul and all that is within me bless His Holy Name!" But how can this be a reality expressed with fullness of joy and not "lip service" if the soul is in a stranglehold trapped by emotional bondage and hurt memories. God is a Spirit and desires that those who worship Him must worship Him in spirit and in truth. *John 4:24.* Emotional issues block the joy and hinder pure worship. In the ongoing process of purifying the heart and renewing the mind we will possess the mind of Christ. "For the Lord will keep him in perfect peace whose mind both it's inclination and character is stayed on Him". *Isaiah 26:3.* We must come to understand that we are the righteousness of God in Christ and that we have right standing in Him. There should therefore be no room for condemnation, doubt or fear. *1John 1:9* tells us that if we freely confess our sins that He is faithful and just to forgive us and to cleanse us of all unrighteousness. Our right standing privilege before the throne lies within this verse.

The mistake many of us make is not keeping short accounts with God. Piling up one transgression upon the other, thinking that it is alright to tread upon the grace of God will cause us to live in defeat. Instead of having a cleansed conscience and enjoying the Presence, grace and fellowship of the Holy Spirit, we will experience condemnation and guilt which is not His will for us. When we come to the throne of grace we will not have confidence to stand before Him and pour out our hearts to Him. You see there is a hardening which can take place in our hearts when we fail to partake of the provision made available for us to be forgiven. We put off repenting and then do something else again and then put off repenting again and again. Hence we are cautioned to urge and admonish and encourage one another every day as long as it is called today so that none of us will be hardened into rebellion against God. *Hebrews 3:13.* O how we need the help of the Holy Spirit so that our hearts will be clean and flowing with the life of Jesus…that He will burn out all that is contrary to His will by the righteous fire of His Love.

"Blessed are the pure in heart: for they shall see God". *Mathew 5:8.* With pure hearts we will see the will of God and understand His plan for us more clearly. Our path will grow brighter from day to day. Removing the clutter and bondage from our lives is the work of the Holy Spirit when we submit to Him. He wants us free, healed and whole. Not bound. He has a perfect plan for our lives, and a shining path for each of us; His thoughts towards us are only good, and not evil. *Psalms 139:17-18.* says that His thoughts concerning us are more numerous than the grains of the sand.

OUTSIDE THE PRISON BUT IN THE PRISON

There are many in the body of Christ who may not own up to being a prisoner, held captive and behind "bars" of low self esteem, emotional wounds, fears of all sorts, habits and past sins and failures. All these are invisible to the human eye but not passed over by our loving Lord.

I was one of those going through the motions Sunday after Sunday in the first eleven years of my conversion, because I did not have the complete understanding of the power of the blood of Jesus to forgive totally and give a new beginning. Neither did I understand the grace and mercy of God.

There are times that we stand aghast in the Body of Christ when we hear of God's people and particularly those in positions of leadership falling into sin. But nothing happens overnight. It takes the enemy a considerable amount of time to really set up a plan for our destruction. He has to study us carefully and come to a crafty conclusion as to where our weaknesses are and where we are most susceptible to fall; in other words he draws up a programme of collected data concerning us . This in no way means that a born again Christian is in any way possessed with a demon! The flesh as we know it, is that fallen nature of man without the Holy Spirit, and will not be redeemed at all. There are sins of the flesh and sins of the spirit, but in each case the temptations of the devil are always what drives a person to rebel against God, being unstrained by the Holy Spirit. We cannot condone sin at any level, but at the same time we must realize that when people struggle within themselves to get rid of certain thought patterns of temptation [which are literal strongholds], destructive habits, and character issues which many times have their root in past experiences they only sink deeper and deeper into satan's snare. There is no room for anyone to boast or to condemn another person. If not for the grace of God we are all one step or one breath away from depravity in any area of life I would say, and this is why we must allow our consciences to be the real preachers on the pulpits of our hearts. The Apostle Paul warned of the real danger of rejecting or thrusting away our consciences which when done leads to making shipwreck of the faith. *1 Timothy 1:19.* We should always ask the Father to help us by the Holy Spirit to have a tender conscience so that we can know when we are going in directions which lead to destruction, because there is such a thing as self deception when we violate our very consciences. Jesus said it this way... "The light of the body is the eye: therefore when thine eye is single, thy whole body also is full of light; but when thine eye is evil, thy body is full of darkness. Take heed therefore that the light which is in thee be not darkness. If thy whole body therefore be full of light having no part dark, the whole shall be full of light, as when the bright shining of a candle doth give thee light" *Luke 11 34-36.* You see when we know that something is wrong from a conscience stand point of view and still proceed to put that wrong deed into action, we numb and violate our consciences; it comes as if we put our minds [which have the capacity to contain our reasoning powers and rational thinking] on hold for the moment, and separate this from the emotions; so that we act purely by what feels good, sounds good or looks good. Sometimes there could be some other subtle pattern of the heart which on the surface appears minor, but what we must realize is that there are no big or little sins. Because we live in a fallen world with a sinful body it is very easy for our hearts to yield in directions which do not please God at any given time if we are not careful. There is no one who can say that they have no sin according to the bible in *1 John 1:10* and *Proverbs 20:9* says "Who can say I have made my heart clean, I am pure from my sin?" All sin whether it is unbelief, doubt, lying, gossip or else has a tendency to eat away at our very souls when left unrepented and cleansed by the blood of Jesus. The fact that we are imperfect beings, it is not that we do not sin or make mistakes, but we must not practice sin or make a commitment to it. The bible says that whoever practices, or commits sin is not a child of God but is of the devil. *1John 3: 6,8,9.* Any pattern of sin left unrepented causes us to have inner intense struggles and disrupts our fellowship with the Lord. Battling and wrestling with secrets is nothing that the enemy of our souls will sit back lightly on. No he will pounce with all viciousness because this plays right into his own backyard. He is the prince of darkness and loves when we operate in the dark. Actually doing so gives him an open door to prevail against us. I have found that we cannot fight thoughts which the enemy brings to us with thoughts of our own. For instance we may sense a raging battle coming against us as he viciously assaults us in our minds, relentlessly; maybe bringing up the past, reminding us of our failures, seeking to make us depressed and hopeless, feelings of unworthiness, strong temptation to draw back into sinful practices, and so many other weapons which he has in his arsenal to use against us. The point to remember here is that he is already defeated and can only come against us with carnal weapons because he is already disarmed by the Lord Jesus Christ, {Colossians 2:15} and we possess spiritual armor and weapons which are mighty through God. Sometimes we may start off resisting him, doing everything we know according to our level of experience with the Lord and we may have some relief, but he comes again and again with the same temptation! What is his motive? He intends to wear us down with the same attack in an effort to get us to wave the white flag in surrender saying "I can't take it any more, I am quitting or "I am just going to give in because God is not helping me!" I am sure that so many people are familiar with this just as I am. I have heard of people who fought in this territory and eventually gave into their feelings and the suggestions of the enemy. This battle or warfare is very real and we all as Christians have to understand this. What should we do in such cases like this? We have to run and keep running to the Lord! We have no match within ourselves against this formidable foe satan, but the Lord Jesus Christ. I know what it is to battle in this arena myself and I can tell you it is extremely serious. We must remember how Jesus handled the enemy's great taunts with the Word of God, "it is written, but also His victories were won because of His complete reliance on His Father and His deep communion with Him all of the time. Even then the bible says that the devil left off tempting Jesus only for a season. That meant that he was coming right back again, so that even when we have victory in one area or another we should remember that satan is surely going to come back once again. We have to develop that same pattern and go running to the Lord for the help that we need and not only during the conflict but by building up on our communion with Him constantly and disciplined study in the word of God. Satan will even try to intimidate us by saying things like…"You can't let anyone in your family know this or don't tell anyone in your church….they will abandon you and put you to shame casting you out". The liar that he is! It is not the will of God for us to struggle in any area of our lives and be defeated. Neither is it His will for us to try in our own strength in secret especially when there are strongholds to be brought down. We must have the help of the Body of Christ. Sometimes a person will need to find someone whom they can be transparent with who will counsel them and pray with them. This will shut the door to the enemy because we should "confess our faults one to another and pray for each other so that we may be healed". When there is obedience to God's word satan has no choice but to leave.

I can say on a personal note that whenever the searchlight of the Holy Spirit has come on any area of my life revealing to me any specific situation which is out of line with the word of God I sense my desperate need of the Lord again and again. It does cause me to humble myself before the Lord and come to the end of my journey of trying to fix my life by covering up pain or sin with band aids which do not heal or bring cleansing. It is only when we are willing to see ourselves in God's light that healing can begin. He gives the grace and creates the willingness in us because He is merciful.

A lost and dying world awaits the manifestation of the sons of God to arise and accept our true position in the kingdom of God and so bring life and hope to them. If we ourselves are in chains how can we announce deliverance to the captives? We cannot pretend to be anything that we are not to this world, but as we walk in the light and allow the Excellency of God's Power to flow through us they will listen as we lift up Jesus. We ourselves will experience the genuine manifestation of God's glory just like the early church did and much more. Jesus wants to be revealed as the risen Christ and as One Who can be touched with the feeling of people's infirmities, and not as a far off God. He is a personal God and stands ready to intervene in the affairs of man. He died for every person on planet earth and He is the same yesterday today and forever...... always responding to those who will put their faith in Him.

In the time in which we live, when the souls of men and women are literally shaking over hell daily, we should be crying out to God daily to take away all our pretending masking and false coverings and make us the people He has planned for us to be. As long as we are in this physical body and in this fallen earth we should continue to cry out to be changed constantly. We must have repeated re-consecrations and rededications with fresh gushings of the Holy Spirit in our lives. If we don't, lukewarmness and hardness will easily settle into our hearts and minds and we will end up living like the rest of the world, instead of like kings and priests unto God.

ONLY JESUS CAN CHANGE A HEART: BUT WE MUST CONFESS

In the book of Genesis 27-28, and 32, there is the story of Jacob who ended up with the blessing of God and in the covenant line up with his grand father Abraham and his father Isaac. Before he could receive the full blessing he had to confess to God the full nature of his name. Names have very significant meanings especially as far as the biblical names are concerned. His name actually had a meaning as most names do and so each time his name was called he identified with the nature and character of that name, causing his actions to correspond accordingly. His name meant trickster, con-artist, swindler, and liar. He ended up stealing the birth right of his older brother Esau through the advice of his mother. As he wrestled with an angelic being one night he refused to let go of the angel saying....."I will not let you go unless you bless me". *Genesis 32:26. NLT. New Living Translation.* The angel asked him "what is your name"? This must have surprised Jacob, for now he had to reveal his character as con artist, swindler and liar. He was made to understand at that time that, that was not his real name...but his name was really Israel- which meant " prince with God".... "for as a prince hast thou power with God and with men, and hast prevailed", verse 28. Jacob experienced a complete transformation of his personality as he exposed himself to a Holy God. The angel smote him on the thigh leaving him with a life long limp, *Genesis 32:32*.

Confession is what most of us lack. The need to be real with God and have Him change us from the inside out, so He can bless us and make us a blessing. Jacob was changed. His moral character went through a metamorphosis as the change occurred on the inside where he struggled with his identity. Read Genesis 29,30 and 31.

The Bible says "and Jacob was left alone". Very often we have to be left alone so that God can deal with us. Surrounded by people all the time can give us the opportunity to not be real and cover up in areas which could impede our spiritual progress and not realize the true purpose of God for our lives. We tend to try to be like everyone else and not heed the individual call of God. Some of us just love to have someone in our company all of the time; if not in person then through a phone conversation. Remember though that being left alone does not necessarily mean that we are alone. Jacob had an angelic ministry accompanying him Genesis 32:1, he had the word of the Lord continually confirmed to him again and again, reminding him that he was going to be protected and that he would return to the land of his forefathers. We too must take heed to the truth of God's word and His promises to us so that we will be willing to submit ourselves to Him unreservedly and allow Him to change us in order that we may fulfill our purpose in the kingdom of God. One thing that I believe I can attest to is that where there are lingering struggles which the Holy Spirit wants to deal with, He will at some time in our walk with Him begin to cause these to surface in one way or another. Whatever the weakness, we have to realize that Jesus is the Author and Finisher of our faith, and God knows the plans that He has for us which are not to harm us in any way; so when we struggle or find ourselves wrestling in any particular area, we must learn to recognize what it is that the Holy Spirit wants to bring to our attention, as His ultimate aim is to help us and transform us to be more Christlike. In such instances I believe we should obey Jesus' command which He gave to the man in the synagogue whose hand was withered......"stretch forth thy hand". *Luke 6:10*. As He did so his hand was restored to wholeness. We must realize that nothing in our lives is a secret to God, for there is no "creature that is not manifest in His sight: but all things are naked and opened unto the eyes of him with whom we have to do". We must expose that struggling area to Jesus so that the Holy Spirit can help us and restore us; it makes no difference what that situation is, He stands ready to help, for that is a part of His wonderful ministry to us. As we draw near to Him in communion and fellowship we will find that He truly is a friend and that we can tell him the most trusted secrets of our hearts and He will not make fun of us or intimidate us in any way. Instead

He will comfort us help us to understand whatever clouds our understanding, make all things clear to us and set us on the right path. He will guide us and show to us what we need to do and as we cooperate with Him Jesus will be glorified in our lives. Every one has something in their lives which has been withered; it may not be a physical withering away but spiritual; battles on the inside, problems, family situations, habits, sins of the flesh, things which keep us weighed down and handicapped from being effective. There are pitfalls and stumbling blocks in many of our lives; areas where we just can't seem to get the victory. Hold everything up to the Lord, every wounded withered situation, for His resurrection power is real and will be released to quicken and restore every department of our lives.

NAME TAGS

Many of us have worn name tags and labels, pinned on us by society, due to whatever we were involved in, in the past. These so called tags associated us with certain types of life styles and behavior which we partook in. When God brings us into our true destiny He changes our moral character from the inside out and gives us a new walk and a new name. Even if people cannot understand what has happened to us and insist on using the same old name tags to connect us to our past, the fact is that God has unhooked us and freed us and all that remains is the limp as a constant reminder of the grace of God or the Hand of God that touched us and freed us. We should never pay too much attention to the limp more than to recognize and praise God for His mercy and His Love to us. Jacob's limp was literally physical. Ours could be in the area of a prolonged illness due to a lifestyle of drug or alcohol addiction, or the practice of immorality. Don't let that be your main focus, for if God in His mercy reached down to touch your heart and change you through the saving grace of His Son and His shed blood on Calvary then he is more than able to bring about whatever changes are necessary for you to live an overcoming life while here on this earth in your physical body.

You must block out the back ground noise of the negative voices of people who have decided who you are, what you should become, and what can be expected of you. When God comes on the scene He wipes away all those false ideas of the past and the character moulds formed by the opinion of others, thereby giving us a new beginning. People do not decide which way we go. God has already decided and awaits our agreement with His plan and our acknowledgement and agreement that we do need Him. There are times in His great sovereignty that He comes to us even when we are not reaching for Him. It is so good to know that each moment and each day we live has already been recorded in His book. *Psalms 139: 16*

Jacob knew that he was promised an inheritance of his grand father Abraham and his father Isaac, but he followed the manipulative advice of his mother and ended up fleeing from his brother Esau in total fear. In other words his mother accessed the situation in her own way and had it not been for the unchangeable word of God he would have been wiped out of the plan of God. Even though the scheme was successful, God had already spoken a Word over Jacob when he was still in his mother's womb that the elder son will serve the younger *Genesis 25:23*. The fact that he was a twin.... and being the last one to be born would not hinder him from being in the covenant line up with Abraham and Isaac with whom God had already established His covenant. His visitation from God caused him to realize who he really was and to fulfill God's word originally spoken about him. God has already spoken His word to all of His children revealing His great plan for our lives. He will not change His mind for He is faithful to complete what He has started.

WE HAVE BEEN REDEEMED BY THE BLOOD OF THE LAMB

Remember that when we are born again we are sealed by the Holy Spirit and God sees us clothed in the righteousness of Jesus Christ! *Ephesians 1:13*.

When I think how much God loves us! He even loves the vilest offender; the backslider who is unsure that he can be forgiven, that one who cannot forget the pain of the past and move on! I would like you to know that God really loves you! Receive His love now and He will have mercy on you.

Jesus went to Calvary's Hill carrying His own cross laden and burdened with the sins of humanity. He was tortured, mocked and scourged and received brutal stripes on His sacred back. Brought to judgement by sinful men, and plucked at the beard till blood flowed. He endured the spitting in His face and a crown of thorns pressed into His Head as He was eventually suspended between heaven and earth........crucified. As His side was pierced He cried out "It is finished"! What powerful words- man's total redemption was accomplished and paid for and man would never be the same again. Glory to God! He took sin, fear, weakness, sickness, disease grief and all the miseries to be expected as a result of sin. The blood He shed did not just cover our sin....it remitted it taking it completely out of the way.

As the Old Testament reflects types and shadows of that which was to be perfected and consummated in Christ, let us take a look at the book of Hebrews. In *Hebrews 10:1* it says "for since the law has merely a rude outline and foreshadowing of good things to come, instead of fully expressing those things, it can never by offering the same sacrifices continually year after year, make perfect those who approach it's altars", verse 2-4. "For if it were otherwise would those sacrifices not have stopped being offered since the worshippers had once for all being cleansed they would no longer have any guilt or consciousness of sins but as it is, these sacrifices annually bring a fresh remembrance of sins to be atoned for because the blood of bulls and goats is powerless to take sins away".

Hebrews 10:12-13. "Where as this One Christ after he had offered a single sacrifice for our sins that shall avail for all time sat down at the right Hand of God then to wait until His enemies should be made a foot stool under His feet". *AMP. Amplified Bible.* Under the Old covenant there was an annual remembrance of sins over and over again., but now in Christ we can come near to God by faith in His blood having our hearts sprinkled and purified from guilt and an evil conscience. *Hebrews 10:22.*

There is no need for the child of God to walk around day after day burdened with a condemned conscience and thoughts of guilt. No one can serve God in this way. When God forgives us, he forgives us entirely. As a matter of fact we see from the scriptures that He has always made a way…. even through the blood of bulls and goats to enable man to be reconciled , forgiven and to have fellowship with Him. The point is that the blood of those animals could not cleanse completely and irradicate sin, but merely covered it. In Christ our sin is completely blotted out by his precious blood! In *Leviticus 16:21-22,* there is the scene of the scapegoat over which the sins of the people were confessed and then this goat was let go in the wilderness to a place of no return. This was God revealing all the while what He would accomplish through Christ. As He takes away the sin He remembers it no more. He blots it out like a thick cloud so that we can stand before Him justified…just as if we had never sinned. As a matter of fact this is just what our position of righteousness means! Being in right standing with God through faith in Christ Jesus and being able to approach God any time any place any where. We must learn to tap into God's provision for our cleansing and quickly repent of anything in our lives which is against His will and His Word.

This is true for those outside of Christ who need to know that they too can receive forgiveness of sins and become children of the Most High God. "For it was God personally present in Christ reconciling and restoring the world to favor with Himself not counting up and holding against men their trespasses but canceling them and committing to us the message of reconciliation of restoration to favor". *2 Corinthians 5:20 . AMP. Amplified Bible.* God had once and for all taken care of the sin problem through Jesus.

The responsibility rests with man....his choice, his will. Will he choose Jesus when he hears about God's love, mercy and all that Jesus was made to suffer for him or will he refuse? God will not force. He has already done all that He could do for every human being on this earth.

I believe that King Solomon after he had been through all his experiences and short comings finally realized and penned these words: "let us hear the conclusion of the whole matter; fear God and keep His commandments: for this is the whole duty of man. For God shall bring every work into judgement, with every secret thing, whether it be good, or whether it be evil". *Ecclesiastes 12:13-14.*

CONDEMNATION

Condemnation and guilt prevents people from receiving anything from the Lord when He is willing to give it to them. Condemnation blocks up and stops up the flow of God's grace and power. This happens when we continue to focus on past sins and mistakes even when God has forgiven us. If we are not watchful we can listen to the voice of guilt which will keep us from putting our trust in Christ. Satan will come by very subtly saying things like "remember what you did yesterday, or last month or even years ago? Do you think that God will let you off the hook?"

When you see yourself as unworthy, unloved and worthless is when you have played right into the hands of the enemy. Conviction which is a completely different thing is the loving work of the Holy Spirit, which ought to lead us to repentance...a change of heart and putting our trust in the Lord Jesus to forgive us. Once we have made a decision to turn completely away from the thing which opposes the will of God for our lives, we can expect His grace and mercy to be manifested in our lives. Condemnation is therefore the work of satan and must not be embraced. This does not take from the law of sowing and reaping which will always be in effect. *Galatians 6:7.* Nevertheless seeds sown in one's past which have left an evil and painful harvest can be uprooted by the power of God's word and the blood of Jesus in the lives of all those who genuinely repent and forsake their sins. God is able to free us completely severing all roots, so when consequences come as a result of sowing and reaping, reach out and trust in the mercy of God. Consequences do not mean that God loves us any less, but that He is true to His word and His character. His Holiness will be vindicated. When the enemy tries to convince us that we are being punished for something in the past which has already been forgiven and cleansed by the blood of Jesus, we must allow the truth of God's word to renounce that lie. Do not come into agreement with the voice of the enemy. God delights in having mercy on us even when we have to face the consequences for our actions. He has promised never to leave us or forsake us. This is good news.

ROOTS

Jesus said "either make the tree sound healthy and good and it's fruit sound, healthy and good or make the tree rotten, diseased and bad and it's fruit rotten diseased and bad. For a tree is judged by it's fruit." *Mathew 12:33. AMP. Amplified Bible* Whatever is produced from a tree has everything to do with the roots of that tree. The branches and leaves draw their sustenance from the sap of the root; so if the root is diseased or unhealthy, the branches, leaves and subsequently the fruit will be unhealthy.

When the same issues in a person's life seem to recur again and again, then this is a sure sign of a root problem which has to be exposed. Plucking away at the branches, leaves and fruit which manifest as a result of a root situation, only leads to constant defeat. The ax has to be laid at the root of that tree and the root exposed to the light of God's truth so that freedom comes. Manifestations of fear, rejection, negativity or low self esteem have their roots hidden and deeply grounded in a person's emotions, and unless dealt with from within there can be no victory.

God created us spirit, soul and body, in that order, and because our bodies have become so attached to this physical realm, we ignore what is taking place within us. We can be all dressed up, and looking really beautiful on the outside, even doing all the correct things and still be wearing "grave clothes" on the inside; still in bondage. Many times it is when people are placed in situations which are demanding and filled with pressure, during an "unguarded moment" [which we have all had at some time] that we see attitudes and personalities that surprise many. Some may even remark "I thought she/he was so spiritual and walking closely with the Lord". Remember even Peter walked closely with Jesus for the space of three years but still cursed and denied Him. Why was this? This was because Peter was not at the time baptized with the Holy Spirit and changed on the inside. There is no record that this happened again after his genuine conversion and experience with the Holy Spirit. It is also important to know also that even though a person is filled with the Holy Spirit it does not mean that he or she is perfect. The soul has the unique ability to always desire gravitating towards the flesh if not continually under the training of the Spirit through the Word of God. The point here is that anyone who is submitted to the Holy Spirit and falls into error is always quick to repent and allow the blood of Jesus to cleanse them; they will not make excuses or try to justify themselves. I believe that this is the stark difference between being spirit filled and walking presumptuously after the flesh!

Problems all have their roots, and unless the root issues are dealt with they tend to recur. These are the lingering odors binding most of us and hindering our true potential. This does not mean that as Christians we are perfect, and never make mistakes, but the reference is to those of us who know we have root problems and refuse to cooperate with the Spirit of God Who is our Helper and lives within us to help us overcome these subtle areas.

I have personally experienced this when dealing with my own inner problems. No matter how hard I tried, there would seem to be a temporary victory or relief in some subtle area, but before long the same thing would return. I would say "Hey I thought I had overcome here, but how come this is still here with me". I went through a series of defeats again and again until the Holy Spirit revealed to me where my real problems were, where the roots were, and how to deal with them through prayer and the application of God's Word. We should also be aware of the fact that if we are not in constant communion and fellowship with the Lord as we should be, that very often little irritants as I call them pop up from time to time. For instance something which you could easily pass over when you are in such close fellowship with Jesus could become a major issue when you are not spending enough time in God's presence as you should be. You could become easily fretful, anxious or careless in your conversation or responses. I have found this to be true in my own personal experiences, and when I get into God' Presence, I begin to see the very same situation from a different standpoint. Then there is a restoration of peace and understanding that comes from the Holy Spirit. Isn't it wonderful to know that we can find help at the throne of grace for every situation we face, and when we are determined to walk to please the Lord He welcomes our quick response to the Holy Spirit's conviction and our desire to be cleansed by His precious blood so that we could move on up to the next level that He has for us!

FALSE COVERINGS

An emotionally wounded person more or less leads a double life. In other words what you see on the outside can be deceiving. Such people can be very defensive and sensitive. The defense mechanism is lifted up as a shield or umbrella. Some one who swells up easily or is unable to take correction many times will be discovered to be a wounded person. They seem to run away when approached about their behavior. The fear of rejection and pain can cause some to live in a shell coming out in the guise of ministry activities or what ever seems favorable to them.

Childhood wounds are the worst because they come a long way into a person's life, affecting their adulthood. Rejection is I believe the highest form of emotional abuse. Growing up in difficult circumstances does affect us, and if we cannot identify what is at the root of the problems we face we would not be healed. In most cases a relationship with God never matures and is hampered, while people look at Him as being hard and unfair, blaming Him for allowing them to go through whatever they went through. In seeking Him for healing, when relief is not instant they view Him as that earthly father or authority figure who abandoned them or forsook them. The wounded child grows into an adult who never really experienced childhood, because satan stole away that privilege before they could reach maturity. Isn't this why Jesus was so intent when He said "suffer the children to come unto me and forbid them not for of such is the kingdom of heaven"? There are instances when such people become adults who maintain their childish patterns in thought, word and deed. This shows a great need for godly parents who should bring their children to Jesus while they are still very young; this provides them with a stable environment. The plan of the devil is to destroy early childhood stages of development while trying to derail God's plan. His intention is to cause young lives to be so emotionally damaged that they may not make it into adulthood successfully; if they do, he seeks to cause the damage to be so devastating that it is close to being beyond repair. We know that he is a liar because our God always has plans for Divine and sovereign repairs for broken lives. There is nothing impossible with Him neither is there any case too difficult for Him.

Where there is an open wound the enemy has the opportunity to pour in bitterness, fear, and unforgiveness due to damaged emotions and memories. God wants to cleanse these open places, close them up with the blood of Jesus and let His anointing flow through.

It is vital for us to understand that we cannot just ignore our hearts and emotions while moving along in hypocrisy. If and when the Holy Spirit puts the search light on some areas of failure in our inner man we must submit to Him and allow Him to help us to obtain the victory. God is concerned with the whole man......spirit, soul and body and His restoration program is wholeness. *1 Thessalonians 5:23* says "And may the God of peace Himself sanctify you through and through [separate you from profane things, make you pure and wholly consecrated to God;] and may your whole spirit and soul and body be preserved sound and complete and be found blameless at the coming of our Lord Jesus Christ [the Messiah."] Verse 24 says "faithful is He Who is calling you [to Himself] and utterly trustworthy and He will also do this by hallowing and keeping you". *AMP. Amplified Bible.* There is the mountain of the Lord in that secret place of the Most High and it is reserved for those who seek to have clean hands and pure hearts. *Psalm 24:4.* The people who know Jesus are a people of destiny and God will fulfill His good promise by completing what He started. He is never at a loss for answers.

UMBRELLAS

Depression and anger are no strange reactions to an emotionally wounded person. These things cannot be covered up. Until we take the umbrellas and band aids off and stop looking to others for help and look only to Jesus the condition will remain unchanged. The wind of the Holy Spirit is blowing and He desires to enter into these secret places of our lives; into the very basement of our hearts. Jesus is concerned with entering into those closed places...those closets where we have stored memories of hurt experiences. He wants to change and transform broken lives. Give Him the chance. You see you can stay under the covers and umbrellas of ministry and be bound; you can go home after a great day at church and lie on your bed under your blanket still crying "why"?

In speaking of umbrellas, here is an illustration! I was in a rain storm on my way to work one day, and I stopped at a nearby convenience store to purchase an umbrella because naturally I thought it would help. Needless to say, the winds took hold of it and it kept swaying almost to leave my hand! It's frame being so fragile. I battled with this as I proceeded on my journey. Finally one fierce gust of wind blew and the umbrella got bent out of shape. When this happened I decided to close what was left of it and just walk through the rain. I realized that I would get to my destination faster without trying to keep the umbrella over my head. I had a rain hat and a coat, so I braved through! The most interesting thing struck me at that time. I was using up so much energy trying to keep this umbrella over me while the wind kept taking it, and I was still getting wet! When I closed the umbrella I moved faster and got to work in a short time while the wind seemed to be less hazardous to me.

The point is that while we may be trying so very hard to keep certain areas of our lives covered with umbrellas, we use up valuable energy. The covering does not hold forever and we become tired and frustrated. The covering does not stand because it is false....it is the false you and not the person God intended. When we close the umbrella of "make belief", and turn our eyes on Jesus, we will reach quickly into His loving arms where He stands ready to heal, restore and anoint us afresh. The eternal God is our refuge and underneath are His everlasting arms. *Deuteronomy 33:27.* This is our eternal destination. From here He sets us on our way. How great is His mercy! When the umbrella is closed on all our human efforts and we embrace His love, we will find that He was there all the time. How much effort is exerted in trying and failing, trying and failing, hoping that some fleshly remedy will work when in fact nothing will work but the blood of Jesus, and the amazing power of God. He is the Lord who heals us. Receive His healing.

There are principalities and powers who are speaking lies in an effort to hinder people from receiving the healing they need.

To the emotionally wounded person who is in search of that missing dad....who feels robbed of being lovingly fathered; who feels neglected; or that one who has been torn and burnt in the fires of abuse, be it physical, mental, verbal or sexual by someone whom you had once looked up to; maybe an authority figure or even a stranger or a spouse.......let these words which the Holy Spirit inspired me to write comfort you in some way.

"The Father you've longed for and cried many nights through,
Is waiting to show His mercy, love and compassion to you!
Sit there no longer, weep no more,
React not in anger or be bitter and sore.
Jesus restores you to your Father above;
He carried your wounds, pain and rejection because of His love.
He'll heal you and wash away every pain and fear,
And restore you to innocence, presenting you faultless in your Father's care.
Come home weary wanderer,
Come home and find your rest,
Come home to Jesus your Heavenly Father cares.
He loves you and has provided a sacrifice complete;
Jesus as Saviour and as Lord where we find rest sitting at His feet.
Turn from the journey that leads to nowhere,
Receive mercy and grace as you bring Him your care.
Walk not in the way of evil men
Whose path lead to sorrow death and hell!
Forgiveness awaits you peace and joy,
Come weary wanderer Jesus is nigh.
How welcome you are at the throne of grace,
Where you'll meet your Heavenly Father face to face!"

STOP THE WANDERING

There are so many people who need to come to Jesus. There are those who once served the Lord and somewhere in their travel broke and cracked in the fires of life; some have refused to be reconciled, and have forfeited the mercy and grace which God has provided. They have lost faith in the power of the blood of Jesus to keep them and restore them and have marched out of God's presence in anger. Some have looked for a place of blame and have adopted the victim attitude relishing in pity parties and remaining on the side lines. Continuing in this way only opens you up to be fine prey for satan, because he is the author of all confusion and destruction. Our Heavenly Father does not delight in our pity parties or in our destruction. He loves us and is awaiting our willing return. Blame often comes in when people refuse to accept their responsibility in any given situation. Actually this comes from the carnal Adamic nature. When Adam fell he blamed Eve and Eve blamed the serpent. They had already lost their communication with God through disobedience, and were in darkness, as they ran into hiding. Just as God came looking for them with those powerful words "Adam where art thou", He is still speaking to those who are in hiding and are blaming others; He is speaking to those fallen areas of the soul because He wants to restore you completely. There are also times that the burdens and pressures of life coupled with disappointments which never seem to end cause some of us to be so hard pressed that if the Lord in His mercy does not place certain people in our lives to help us through those difficult seasons some of us will hardly make it through to the end. Life can be difficult and Jesus said that it would be, as he foretold of tribulations which we would all have to face at some time in our lives; but He wants us to be of good cheer for He has already overcome the world and deprived it of power to harm us. He has us covered in our Father's love and sheltered by His precious blood.

WELCOME TO THE SCHOOL OF FORGIVENESS

Character is never something which can be changed over night or automatically. It is the constant work of the Holy Spirit, with our cooperation of course which shapes and moulds us into the image of Christ. Whatever areas of testing, trial or circumstance which God allows, no matter how painful and difficult will always be worked out in such a way that Jesus is glorified, and we are changed to be more like Him.

Forgiveness therefore is an individual responsibility which God desires to discipline us in, and can never be based on the other party's actions. We cannot look to see changes in the other person before we decide to forgive and release the issues involved to God.

Forgiveness is based only on the finished work of the cross. The story Jesus told of the unmerciful servant in *Mathew 18: 21-35*, comes to mind. Peter first asked a question seeking to find out how many times he should forgive someone who offends him. Peter had a preconceived idea of how many times he thought a person should be forgiven.....seven times Peter thought was enough. Jesus' reply to him was that forgiveness cannot be limited to seven times but to seventy times seven.......meaning that there is no end to forgiveness. I know someone very well who explained to me that she was sexually abused by her step father. She was very bitter and unforgiving and in the natural who would not be? Obviously she was very emotionally wounded. I identified with her by letting her know that one of the first steps which she needed to take was to forgive the person involved. She went on to painfully say that she had tried to do so several times but found it to be very difficult and came up short over and over again. I was quite familiar with this ritual of trying to forgive, but when I told her that forgiveness must not be based on the other person's actions, or whether or not they owned up to being wrong, she confessed to be struggling in this particular area. The struggle we all go through. "Should I forgive you? I demand justice and vengeance! I demand you to fall down before me and say you're sorry so every one will know that it was not my fault. I demand you to own up to being wrong because I have been wronged by you." The foundation of all forgiveness is based on our believing and understanding God's all powerful love. I believe that we have all traveled on this road of holding grudges and not forgiving others for it can happen in little things or most definitely in bigger issues. We live in this fallen world where people will behave in a manner that is unkind or unjust or just plain cruel. We also must know that forgiveness should be separated from reconciliation. We have to choose to forgive based on what we know of the finished work of the cross and our having a deep understanding of it. However reconciliation is quite different because in some cases it is not at all possible, applicable or workable.

With Jesus as our example we can see that He taught on forgiveness "forgive us our debts as we forgive our debtors". "For if we do not forgive others their trespasses our heavenly Father will not forgive us our trespasses." *Mathew 6 12-14.*

It is not the easiest lesson to learn and so many of us fail in this area. This is why God does not want us to rely on ourselves but on His Holy Spirit to enable us to do what He said. When I received a deeper revelation of the cross, it was only then that I was able to release and forgive people freely, and this of course is on going as a way of life for me and should be for all of us. There is no end to it for Jesus Himself said that offenses will always come, *Luke 17:1* but we have to decide whether we will take the offence or not. I realize that offence is like something offered on a platter by the devil who knows the state of our flesh. We have to decide whether we will take and eat from his table or whether we would eat from the table which the Lord prepares for us in the presence of the enemy. *Psalm 23:5* We must depend on God's grace. Without this there can be no wholeness for emotionally wounded people. The Holy Spirit wants to help each person individually… whether you are a child, a young person or an adult. He knows just what to do and where to start. He also knows how to move us along in stages through His healing program until wholeness is accomplished. All He needs is our willingness and our cooperation.

"Therefore is the kingdom of heaven likened unto a certain king which would take account of his servants. And when he had begun to reckon, one was brought unto him that owed him ten thousand talents. But as much as he had not to pay, his lord commanded him to be sold and all that he had and payment to be made. The servant therefore fell down and worshipped him saying "Lord, have patience with me and I will pay thee all. Then the lord of that servant was moved with compassion, and loosed him and forgave him the debt. But the same servant went out and found one of his fellow servants which owed him a hundred pence and he laid hands on him and took him by the throat, saying "pay me that thou owest". And his fellow servant fell down at his feet and besought him saying, "have patience with me and I will pay thee all." But he would not but went and cast him into prison, till he should pay the debt. So when his fellow servants saw what was done, they were very sorry, and came and told unto their lord all that was done. Then his lord after that he had called him, said unto him "O thou wicked servant. I forgave thee all that debt because thou desirest me. Shouldest not thou also have had compassion on thy fellow servant, even as I had pity on thee? And his lord was wroth and delivered him to the tormentors till he should pay all that was due unto him. So likewise shall my heavenly Father do also unto you, if ye from your hearts forgive not everyone his brother their trespasses". *Mathew 18: 25-35.*

The tormentors can come in various ways if we keep walking in unforgiveness and willfully take hold of offences. There is no peace in that way of life. Jesus paid our debts in full. He took our sin [the sin we were born with for we have all been born in sin and shapen in iniquity] *Psalm 51:5* and the sins we committed through life and continue to commit. He so freely forgave us and so it is mandatory that we forgive others. He gives us the ability to forgive and to love because He works in us both to will and to do of His good pleasure. *Philippians 2:13.*

I repeat we must be willing because forgiveness is an act of our will. God will not force us or excuse us. If there is no willingness on our part to receive God's grace and mercy which is available to us through the work of the Holy Spirit, we will not be delivered or be able to understand the power of forgiveness. For every thing we will receive from God in any area of our lives we must be willing to listen and obey the Holy Spirit's leading, teaching and counsel. He is so very merciful. He knows how we hurt when our lives have been bruised and battered by sin's dominion in the lives of others. There are sometimes and more often than few, that the abuser or wrong doer may never repent or show remorse of any kind. Some people are so hardened by sin and demonic blindness that they are unwilling to admit to wrong doing and accept the love of God. There are other times that the wrong doer may be waiting to hear the words *"you are forgiven"* so they could be released into God's love.

This is not easy in the natural but goes a long way in the spirit realm when acted upon. The spirit realm dominates everything in this life and this is where everything begins. This is the reason why we must depend on the Holy Spirit. There is no way that any of us can look at an abuser in the eye and say "I forgive you" in our own strength. We have to be led by the Holy Spirit and He knows the way and the precise timing. It may take some people years to forgive, and for some the duration may be much shorter. Meanwhile some people may want to prolong the process because they do not want to let go and desire to relish in an atmosphere of pain for as long as possible. Some think that if they let go and trust God that the other party gets off too easily, but we must remember the tormentors in that story and that no one gets off. We must not try to collect a debt for the debt has already been paid by Jesus. None of us really deserve His love and forgiveness yet He freely pardoned us. The debt we owed for our sin and the price Jesus paid to ransom and redeem us cannot be compared to anything we suffer here in our pilgrimage on this earth sometimes in such brutal ways. Until a wounded person understands this clearly they will not be willing to go on to receive all that God has for them.

The servants in the parable could not pay their debts. The situation there was the vast difference in the amounts owed and the both servants 'cry for mercy. The one who owed such a great amount and knew he could in no way in his life time pay received mercy but was unable to show mercy to the one who owed him so little and was unable to pay. He completely forgot that mercy was shown to him from his lord, so that he would do the same to his fellow servant. Where did this action of his cause him to end up? in the prison of torment. He knew that he could never in his life time pay off the vast amount of money which he owed, yet he begged for time to pay. He received a debt cancellation from his lord which was the only thing the master could do which would release him. Isn't it the same with us? Can we ever repay the Lord for His sacrifice made to set us free from sin's dominion? This is the point of forgiveness. If we really know the debt that we owed and the fact that we could never pay it ever in our entire life time, but received a cancellation of our sin debt through the blood of Jesus, we will really see the need to forgive others and release them from our hearts rather than holding on to them and being tormented. What when you are the offending party? You will have to accept your role and responsibility in the matter and seek ways to compensate the offended party in some way as you seek the wisdom of God. If you have sought their forgiveness and for some reason they have not accepted this offer as genuine you should wait in prayer until the Holy Spirit works in the person's heart and gives them the grace to accept forgiveness from you. It would be a great tragedy for you to bear the weight of condemnation and guilt day in and day out for what you have done when you have repented to God and sought their forgiveness. Move on in the purpose of God and do whatever it takes to be conformed to the character of Christ. Eventually you will receive grace from God and He will move in the lives of others bringing peace, healing and restoration for we all offend others in some way all the time. The immoral woman in the bible came in behind Jesus, with the only thing she had left beside her sinful life which was a beautiful jar of expensive perfume. She proceeded to pour the perfume on His feet, while bathing His feet with her tears. She was desperate for a new way of living and after hearing that Jesus was the Messiah who came to set captives free she sought to be freed from the sin that held her captive.....weeping and broken she had no words to offer Him. Here Jesus again referred to two different people who owed money; one a greater sum than the other. Neither could pay their creditor and he forgave them both. The one whose debt was greater was more grateful and loved him more, while the other who had little to be cancelled loved less. This woman's sin debt due to immorality was great but Jesus said to her "your sins are forgiven". *Luke 7:36-50.* These are powerful words. He sent this woman away knowing that she was forgiven and in peace........which meant wholeness and completeness in exchange for her broken life. Jesus is called the *Prince of Peace, and the first message of the angels who announced His birth was peace on earth good will to men.* It is the same with us, for we have entered into wholeness when Jesus brought us into salvation. If Jesus has affirmed to you that your sins are forgiven, knowing how great a debt you have owed, then, because of your love for Him Who alone could pardon your sin why not in turn forgive others? He has spoken often in His word about peace, forgiveness and wholeness. Maybe we need a new assurance of this truth from the Holy Spirit, to reassure us that our sins have been forgiven. If we have not yet understood through the penetrating work of the Holy Spirit that our many, many sins have been forgiven we will go around as debt collectors time and again! As we travel through life in this fleshly body we tend to forget. Even as we take for granted the grace of God, and fall short in several areas in our walk with God we fail to live a life in humble repentance. There are people who do not think that it is necessary to be repentant in small things more so in bigger things. They fail to respond to the conviction of the Holy Spirit and have the blood of Jesus cleanse them. It is a deception to think that all we needed was to accept Jesus in our hearts at conversion and then continue to go on our way. Failure to be cleansed by the blood of Jesus and to appropriate His sacrifice daily in our lives could cause us to become hardened and not live in the process of sanctification. This obviously leads to us not realizing the need to forgive others when they have wronged us, because we fail to realize that when we confess our sins He if faithful and just to forgive our sins and cleanse us from all unrighteousness. *1 John 1:9.* How can we claim to love the Lord our God with all our hearts, souls, minds and strength, and our neighbor as ourselves, [which is the greatest commandment], when we remain in total violation of this command?

Therefore we should never demand a payment from another person. Rather than leaving room for the tormentors we should be saying like the Psalmist, "What shall I render to the Lord for all His benefits towards me? I will lift up the cup of salvation and deliverance and call on the Name of the Lord". *Psalm 116:12-13.* What is the cup of salvation? It includes recognizing God's love, His mercy and grace, so that even when your debtor refuses to acknowledge his or her wrong and fall at your feet confessing to you, remember that the cup of salvation can be lifted up as you call upon the Name of the Lord, and you can draw fresh water freely from the wells of salvation to heal and make you whole. This is of greater value than to continue in a wounded state. Besides this if you have become a Christian, and the wounds of the past continue to haunt you because of an unforgiving attitude, you will find that your prayers are hindered. The word says "If I regard iniquity in my heart, the Lord will not hear me. *Psalm 66:18.* God is able to work all things together in our lives for good if we would but trust Him completely and cleave to His word. The bible says that suffering produces patience and endurance, which in turn produces character. Many times we want a quick way out of the problem but all the while God knows what He wants to accomplish for His glory. He will take what has been so very painful and traumatic in our lives and weave it into a tapestry so full of His grace, compassion and love, which would bless the world. Who gets the glory? *JESUS.* There is no person who has truly gone through levels of trials and suffering and has continued to trust Jesus who cannot be a blessing in return to others. God is looking for people whom He can use to set the captives free and bring His healing power to heal the broken hearted. Has your heart been broken? God wants to make you whole and mend your life so you can in turn be a vessel of mercy to someone who would be going through the same situation which He brought you through. Don't run from the problem! Remain on the Potter's wheel and see what a marvelous vessel He can make out of your seemingly ruined life. Bread can be shared when it is broken and blessed to feed the multitudes. Our God is not looking for great people or even good people, for only He is good and great; the people He is really looking for are the true worshippers who are willing to worship Him in spirit and in truth, who bear the marks and scars of Calvary, to show to this world his everlasting love and mercy so that they might believe.

God is greater and in His mercy He can place so many wonderful people in our lives to help us along the way, but we must never refuse to be comforted. Doing this can cause you to attract spirits of sorrow and grief while you resist the work of the Holy Spirit. Continuing to rehearse and keep a record of the past in the private files of our minds while seeking solace within ourselves or from others with the "woe is me" attitude can be very dangerous. If we stop rehearsing it God will reverse it. Jesus said to love our enemies and even to pray for them. *Mathew 5:44.* You can hardly hold something against someone in unforgiveness while praying for them. As long as you pray you leave the way open for God's love to flow through and be released breaking the hold of the powers of darkness. The Lord turned around Job's captivity when he prayed for his friends. The enemy cannot hold you captive to any situation when you obey the Lord and begin to pray for your enemies. He is afraid of the love of God and cannot function in an atmosphere where God's love prevails.

IN HIS PRESENCE

There are no quick fixes. People should not be deceived into thinking that as they go to the altar during a service or attend a few counseling sessions that it ends there. This is a false sense of security. For every situation and in this instance to address the emotionally wounded you must allow the Holy Spirit to lead you into a disciplined life in the Presence of God. Prayer meetings worship services, bible studies and fellowships must be harmonized with that private quiet time in His Presence. God wants us to know and experience His love in deep and intimate ways. He wants us to come and draw near to Him through His Word and allow His Holy Spirit to teach us and minister to us during those times of being alone with Him. This does not in any way mean that He can't use a variety of means to speak to us. I have had the Lord speak to me and give me specific directions for my life and that of my family through someone's testimony. God is not limited, but He wants us to be in an environment of practicing His Presence all the time. You know the woman at the well. I am sure that every bible reading believer knows about her. After her encounter with the Lord Jesus she ran to the town to tell everyone about the Man who told her everything about her life. The people gathered together to see who this prophet was. They listened carefully to what Jesus said and then told the woman "now we believe, not because of thy saying; for we have heard Him ourselves , and know that this is indeed the Christ, the Saviour of the world." *John 4:42. King James Bible.* Here we see that testimony is not enough because unless we have a genuine encounter with the true and living God in the name of the Lord Jesus Christ through the Holy Spirit, we cannot live by someone else's testimony. We must hear Him for ourselves through the convicting power of the Holy Spirit, and believe and receive all that He has for us by faith in Him. There are some who only come near to Him on Sundays, or maybe during a mid week service, while ignoring Him and His counsel all the time. If you really want to experience the victory you will have to learn to wait in His presence continually. God can also speak to us and give us a direct word or instruct us in any place when we are in tune with His

Holy Spirit. He wants us to pick up our bibles and get to know Him and His ways and dealings. The Presence of God is like manner. There is no one time experience which will make us all satisfied enough to not need to return to Him, for a fresh encounter. We must keep going to Him for His mercies are new every day. There is a fresh supply for each new day. We sow to the Spirit to reap eternal benefits when we learn to put God's word first place in our lives. The Word will continue to rise grow and increase as we fellowship with the Lord. This gives us great boldness and confidence before the throne and assures us that our prayers are being heard and answered even before we receive the outward manifestation.

Reading the bible carelessly, flipping through the pages mechanically will not benefit us in any way. This only results in head knowledge most of the time. The word of God will continue to remain on the pages of the bible until we allow the Holy Spirit to lead us. There are passages of scripture which will directly apply to situations which we go through at various times and the Holy Spirit may want us to focus there at some given point in time so we must be sensitive to His direction. As we seek His face that word will become spirit and life to us and as we go to the throne of grace we go with God's word in our mouths, knowing that He has spoken to us. There are times when portions of truth stand out boldly before us and we know that He has spoken. It becomes like a highlighter brightens up a verse or some verses of scripture which the Holy Spirit wants to make clear to us. Isn't God wonderful to love us in this way? He is our teacher. The word of God tells us to get wisdom and with all that we get, get understanding. We have to make a decision that we do need the Lord, and will draw close to him in fellowship and dependence on Him alone. If we seek Him we will find Him; and we must ask Him for a promise which covers our situation and anchor our faith there. There is no other way to the path of victory.

The Holy Spirit longs to make Jesus real to every one of us, as One Who cares and is concerned with the minutest details of our lives. Not just as the God Who died for our sins so we could escape hell, and is now up in heaven looking down at suffering humanity not knowing what to do. Jesus is able to heal and deliver us any time. All we have to do is to be willing to come to Him.

"Come to me all you who labor and are heavy laden and I will cause you to rest. [I will ease and relieve and refresh your souls.] Take My yoke upon you and learn of Me for I am gentle and humble in heart, and you will find rest, [relief ease and refreshment and recreation and blessed quiet] for your souls. *Mathew 11:28-29.AMP. AMPLIFIED BIBLE.*

There can be no experience of abundant life if we have memories haunting us from the past. We discover the truth about God's nature and character, _pamela b h victor_

and we discover ourselves and who He says we are as we fellowship around the word of God in prayer.

You see for the wounded and those suffering from hurt memories of the past, you must realize that your perception of God has been distorted leaving you with a false perception even of your self. Staying in God's presence helps us to realize that the person we thought we were all our lives has been changed into the person He created for His own glory, and our worship becomes spontaneous. He heals the broken hearted and binds up the wounds. He leads the prisoners and captives to everlasting freedom. It all happens in the secret place of His presence. There is no other way. In the reverse we can develop an attitude towards God and keep Him out of our lives and future. When situations and circumstances occur which are painful we could become like Mary the sister of Lazarus who said "Lord if You had been here my brother would not have died." [We may say [Lord how could you have allowed such an evil thing to happen to me when You have all power to have prevented it? How could you have allowed my dad, my mom that stranger, that family friend to do such a thing to me? How could You have let my child die? How could you have let me down?] These are questions that we all ask from time to time. We are so prone to ask the Lord these questions. Meanwhile the Lord is asking us "do you believe that I AM? _I AM_ not the I was or the I will be, but _I AM THE I AM; I AM_ whatever you need now; _I AM_ here now in your present ready to take you into your beautiful future if you will allow Me. Jesus wants us to know that He is walking with us through the suffering NOW, and though we ask questions which He may choose not to give us answers to, or we make rash statements towards Him depending on our view of the circumstance at the time. He still says "fear thou not for I am with thee: be not dismayed for I am thy God. I will strengthen thee; yea I will help thee, yea, I will uphold thee with the right hand of my righteousness. Behold all they that were incensed against thee shall be ashamed and confounded: they shall be as nothing; and they that strive with thee shall perish. Thou shalt seek them and shall not find them, even them that contended with thee: they that war against thee shall be as nothing, and as a thing of nought." _ISAIAH 41:10-12._ In all our afflictions He is afflicted. _Isaiah 63:9._

MOVE ON

Inability to get past the past will leave us with a Lazarus stinking in our hearts killing us one day at a time with the poisonous toxins which flow from dead issues. Every time we think about the situation tears flow out from this place. The words we speak flow out of this same wounded heart because out of the abundance of the heart the mouth speaks. The poisons of emotional abuse never affect only the abused but flow out to others. People act out in ways towards others, even those they love and not know why they do it; they don't know what motivates them because they have never been able or willing to face and process the stuff that happened to them in the past. It all just gets swept 'under the carpet' and left there for several years. Fear torments such a person because they will always be doing everything possible to keep everything under cover. Until we let Jesus see where we have laid the Lazarus of our past, buried deep within the cave of our hearts and allow Him into the tomb of circumstances which led to the burial, there is no restoration healing or wholeness. He wants us to remove the stone, the covering which blocks His healing and His power so that He can call forth those dead issues. Wrapped in grave clothes they will have to obey Him just as the wind or the sea or the devil himself and come forth falling powerless at His feet never to be a part of our lives again.

THERE IS NO NEED TO FEAR.

God has not given to us a spirit of fear so we need not be afraid of Him. I once had a fear of God, but it was not a reverential fear. It was a fear which the devil oppressed me with due to my past sins. It became so bad that when I went to God in prayer I felt He would not answer me. I prayed and prayed but not with the intimacy of a child of God who knows He is their Father. As it were I remained in the outer court begging to be heard, and using all the wrong words in my prayer. [This was of course a reflection of the way I related to my earthly father and the way he related to me. I silently begged for him to love me and accept me and to forgive me whenever I did wrong.] All the while I did not recognize that I was welcome in the Holy of Holies. Staying far off results in a clouded vision and an inability to focus correctly. When God gave the Ten Commandments to Moses in the book of Exodus chapter 20 the Israelites were terrified at the sight of the thunderings and lightnings which their eyes saw and begged Moses to not let God speak to them Himself. They could not go near the mountain which God manifested Himself on and fear gripped them. God is altogether holy and will never change His mind about who He is, but as the law came through Moses, grace and truth came through the coming of Jesus Christ and we can come boldly and fearlessly into His Presence. Grace has been given to mankind to come to Him through the sacrificial blood of Jesus Christ. Staying in the Presence of God means pressing; it involves determination and serious decisions to stay there until we have the victory and to continue. It is the only place where we can fight the good fight of faith. It is written "the just shall live by faith but if any man draw back, my soul has no delight or pleasure in him." *Hebrews 10:38.* We cannot afford to draw back in fear or revert to the past, but we must in faith keep pressing on. *Psalm 18:31-33* says "for who is God except the Lord, or who is a Rock save our God, the God Who girds me with strength and makes my way perfect. He makes my feet like hinds' feet able to stand firmly or make progress on the dangerous heights of testing and trouble He sets me surely on my high places." *AMP. AMPLIFIED BIBLE.* God will give us strength when our strength is failing. He will under gird us when we sense failure or discouragement, and give us everything we need as we begin to climb that mountain toward our restoration. We will never be alone so get in the press and stay in the press.

You enter into presumption when you decide to walk out of your Father's care and protection. The curse and all it's repercussion awaits you. The Psalmist cries "keep back thy servant from presumptuous sins. Let them not have dominion over me." *Psalm 19:13*. People have weak areas in their lives! Areas of the soul which have not been surrendered to God. You may be slipping and falling again and again, because of a weakness and a besetting sin. Do not give up or faint in your mind thinking that God will not restore or deliver you. You need to continue in the word, seek counsel, or what ever other direction the Lord will lead you into. Do not hide these areas from Him or think He does not care. More so do not try to battle in your own strength. You must be prepared to bring every weight and besetting sin to Him again and again, looking unto Jesus the Author and Finisher of our faith. He began our new life in faith and will allow us to finish in faith if we do not faint and give up. Keep running to the blood of Jesus and to the throne of grace; keep going to the altar again and again if you need to but do not give up and throw in the towel, allowing that sin to take root in your life where you decide to practice it as a way of life. This leads to a lascivious pattern of sin which grows and grows and takes over the entire person after a while. The Bible says that sin when full grown brings forth death. *James 1:15*. We should hate that sin, and let the devil and your flesh which is his workshop know that you are not giving up. Jesus said that if we want to be His disciples we must pick up our cross and follow Him, hating our own lives and those things which stand in the way of His fullness. Let your heart be always tender before God and you will see those weaknesses swallowed up by His resurrection life. Perseverence is a fruit of the Spirit and we must persevere in order to overcome.

"And Elisha said unto him, take bow and arrows and he took unto him bow and arrows. And he said to the king of Israel put thine hand upon the bow. And he put his hand upon it: and Elisha put his hands upon the king's hands. And he said, open the window eastward. And he opened it. Then Elisha said shoot. And he shot. And he said the arrow of the Lord's deliverance, and the arrow of deliverance from Syria: for thou shalt smite the Syrians in Aphek, till thou hath consumed them. And he said take the arrows. And he took them. And he said to the king of Israel, smite upon the ground. And he smote thrice, and stayed. And the man of God was wrought with him, and said, thou should have smitten five or six times; then hast thou smitten Assyria till thou hast consumed it: whereas thou shalt smite Syria but thrice. *2 Kings 13:15-19. King James Bible*. This scripture proves that when there are stubborn areas and strongholds in our lives, even after we have come to Jesus, our determined purpose should be to not rest in a place of indifference and comfort until we have the ultimate victory. Being indifferent and careless is much different to resting in the Lord and in His word. You see, our spirit has been redeemed and recreated having come alive to God in Christ, but the fallen areas of the soul still do exist. When there are habits and besetting sins we need not be casual or compromising to develop an attitude by saying "well, that's how I am". This is the flesh speaking and not the Spirit of Christ. He never saved us to remain just how we were before we were saved. This actually frustrates the grace of God. God's full intention is to work in our lives through various means until we are conformed to the image of His Son. How else can we bless this world and show forth the power of the gospel? There are areas in our lives which we have to pray through more than a quick prayer or try to get someone to lay hands on us or get a prayer of agreement in a prayer line or at the altar. We cannot have a microwave situation where we think that we are not responsible for the truth we receive from the word of God, and we must allow the Holy Spirit to work in our hearts and to change us. Truth sanctifies or separates us from the things of the flesh, the world and the devil which try to drag us down. Certain thought patterns or other strongholds must be penetrated by the Spirit of God before they actually lose their power over us. Our willingness to be transparent before the Lord and turn from whatever it is that besets us and prevents us from doing the will of God and making an eternal difference is the key. Some of us are habitual liars, or gossips. And I would just like to interject a word about gossip. A person who gossips is definitely not whole in themselves. If tearing down another person gives you pleasure then something is definitely wrong in your emotional system. This is a destructive habit and destroys the people whom it is launched against in a most painful way while bringing the offender to a place of degeneracy and unfruitfulness. If our relationship with the Lord is in good standing then how is it possible to go against someone whom He died for or who belongs to Him in such vicious ways? Along with gossip is the favorite companion of slander for they go hand in hand. Gossipers never include themselves when spreading rumors about others, but instead proceed to say what they heard from other sources. All of it is with the full intention to tear down and destroy the work of God. The one who receives the poison of gossip becomes just as defiled as the carrier. "A wicked doer giveth heed to false lips and a liar giveth ear to a naughty tongue." *Proverbs 17:4.* Others are full of pride, jealousy and other works of the flesh including bad attitudes. Some may just have a wandering and uncommitted heart, or lacking in love and compassion towards others. Whereas others may find themselves searching, especially in the way of relationships and continually coming up short because they have not yet found soundness or wholeness in themselves or in a developed relationship with the Lord. This is a dangerous area!

Bitterness and malice when allowed to take root will eventually cause you to come to a place where you could find no place of repentance, recovery or restoration like in the case of Esau, when it festers without seeking cleansing. Not that God is unwilling to forgive us but we can allow these things to take up the place in our lives which belong to Him; in other terms we could forfeit our true birth right as sons and daughters of the Most High God in replacement for carnality. The bible says that bitterness has a root and so causes many people to be defiled, for the person who finds themselves in the grip of this evil is full of poison. They proceed to spread this poison to others by way of conversation regarding a matter which has upset them, in order to get the approval agreement or sympathy of unsuspecting persons. A bitter person lacks peace and in this pattern of misery they seek to get others to lose their peace also.

Many times you do not get the victory with one quick prayer and then be on your way. It takes discipline, and character is not formed overnight. Sometimes we see someone who is spiritually successful and being blessed by the Lord and we would like to be like them; but you can be sure that they did not get there by being air lifted or lacking discipline or by quick fixes. They may have come through so many hard knocks and schools of Holy Spirit, failures and deep lessons to learn as well as painful trials and testings. We all know what it is to have besetting sins in our past and as for me the scripture above in *2 Kings,* has and will always be a blessing to me. God helped me as I believed Him and went to Him again and again, until I had the victory over those places. God is still working on me so do not be misled into thinking that I am saying that I have arrived, because the truth is that none of us have or can make such a claim, but I am certainly on my way upwards, pressing towards the mark for the prize of the high calling of God in Christ Jesus. I refuse to draw back or become stagnant. "Our way is not that of those who draw back to eternal misery and [perdition] and are utterly destroyed. But we are of those who believe [and cleave to and trust and rely on God through Jesus Christ the Messiah] and by faith preserve the soul. *Hebrews 10:39. AMP .Amplified Bible.* So we must therefore keep pressing forward striving for the victory, wholeness and soundness until it is fully accomplished by the Holy Spirit. What we do have to realize though is that the closer we walk with the Lord the more we will realize how much we need Him as we would see areas in our own lives which are not in line with His word, and the more we will be disciplined by Him, for whom the Lord loves He corrects! We should never, especially in the present day that we live, where we all do know that the coming of the Lord is truly drawing nigh and our salvation is nearer than when we first believed think of drawing back or building our altars thinking there is no more for us to attain to in God. There is always another level to which we must attain as long as we live in this earth, and the plan of God will continue to unfold in our lives as long as we seek Him diligently. He cannot perfect our flesh, but He does require us to walk in the Spirit through the word and depend upon Him. You see if you really desire to be conformed into the image of Christ, and this is your heart's cry, you will want to get rid of all that blocks His power from flowing through you and prevents the world from seeing His glory. The closer we walk with Him the more we will discover areas in our lives to be surrendered, because we live in a flesh body which seeks to oppose everything the Holy Spirit desires to do in us. You will not want to settle for just regular church attendance, listen to messages preached again and again and have no intention of applying truth to your life. This is deception actually because we are cautioned to not be hearers of the word only but be doers not deceiving ourselves. We will be held accountable for what we have heard in the way of truth, and for failure to walk in the light which has been given to us, for to whom much is given much is to be expected. Truth heard must be applied or else it does us no good. The moment we get caught up in other things, even though they may not necessarily be sinful things there is an open place for us to become careless, and callous concerning the things of God; and before long we would lose our fervor for Him, leading eventually to those same former sins and fleshly desires to become active in our lives. All it takes is to take our eyes off of Jesus… stop reading the word of God as we should, give up on consecrated prayer time and fellowship and move out of the place where He has put us we can be swept away by the current of the world, the devil and the flesh! You see it's either life in and through the Word of God or life in the world. Any move away from the things of the Lord lead to the downward pull. It is one thing to slip in an area and to repent and get up quickly, which is what we should do. There should be no lapse in time where this is concerned. When we leave our lives open to habits whether it's an attitude, or strife or even more grave areas of sin [remembering that sin is sin and it does all matter with the Lord], it causes a hole as it were in our relationship with Him, and a hole in our spiritual lives. Just as leprosy and cancer eat out at a person's life until they cease to exist, so does sin in any form. The bible says it brings forth death. It is not that we do not sin but we should not practice sin. This is why God made such a great provision for us all through the precious blood of Jesus Christ. Let us make use of what He has provided and run to the blood all of the time so that we may receive forgiveness.

THE RUSH HOUR.

We live in an hour where everyone is in a mad rush hoping to reach the top while searching for quick answers and solutions. The ways and means which most people are using to accomplish things by speedy method only leads to the way back down. The microwave age mentality is destroying many, because if we are all not careful we would end up living just for the moment without a care about eternity. No thought about the coming of the Lord for us. It is a time of instant gratification and help yourself gimmicks which is the message from the world. Many are caught in this cycle and living for eternity is the furthest thing on their minds, and yes even Christians are many times overtaken. We should remember that we are really eternal beings and we are only here to fulfill the purpose of the Lord Jesus Christ until His soon return or until we have completed all of our assignments planned by the Lord and He chooses to call us home. Each day that is given to us is a day which has already been recorded by God the Father in His book whereby we should be walking out His plan for our lives. As the people of God, our chief concern should only be to fulfill our calling as we run our course and race with determination to complete it. Remembering that we will all stand before the Lord at the judgment seat so it behooves us to live carefully, watchfully and walking in the fear of the Lord daily as we look for His appearing. At that time the only thing that will matter will be what we did for Jesus and the kingdom of God during our stay here.

Waiting on the Lord causes us to renew our strength; to mount up with wings as eagles; to run and not be weary, to walk and not faint. *Isaiah 40:31*. We can ride above the storms of life on the high places of testing and be victorious. Because *Psalm 23* tells us that there is a table laid before us from which we can eat. What the enemy meant for evil against us is shown openly to him as folly as God spreads a table out for His people where healing and restoration are included on the menu. We are invited to relish and feast on the abundance of His house and He causes us to drink from the streams of His pleasures. *Psalm 36:8-9.*

In the light of His word we see Him high and lifted up. We are led in paths of righteousness for His Name's sake. Jesus leads us out of the past into the glorious future he has for us, and gives us rest in the green pastures of His Word. The more we stay in His presence the more we will sense His direction. The more we continue in His word the more the anointing will be released to destroy every yoke and remove burdens. Here is where our minds are renewed and our souls are restored. Our heavenly Father also deals with us in the quiet places of His presence. Sons and daughters receive chastisement, while judgment is reserved for the sinner who refuses to repent and receive Jesus as his Lord and Saviour. Thank God that He has called us to be His own so that as we live in this earth we seek to honor Him every day of our lives with eternity constantly on our minds. The one thing that we should always remember is that the higher we go up the more humility we should ask the Holy Spirit to produce within us because any thing less can lead to a solid crashing back down as we see so many times over. Moving higher should always make us aware of our inability to sustain ourselves and our constant need should be to stay close to the Lord. True promotion comes from the Lord in the life of the Christian and so when we experience it we should be running to Him continually for strength and wisdom and sustenance.

JESUS THE FOUNTAIN OF LIFE.

"But whoever takes a drink of the water that I will give him shall never no never be thirsty any more; but the water that I will give him it shall become a spring of water welling up flowing, bubbling, continually within him unto into and for eternal life. *John 3:14. Amplified Bible.* The water from Jesus the fountain of life leads to eternal life. The woman who Jesus spoke those words to had been trying to find satisfaction in the arm of flesh through relationships. She had five husbands and then found herself living carelessly with the sixth guy. Had she not met Jesus who discerned her need she would have gone through life searching for that which could not satisfy the thirst of her soul. When her soul came in contact with living water and her way of life was exposed she dropped her water bucket and began running through the town telling everyone that she had now found satisfaction......the Man who told her everything about her life and who offered her the only solution to quench her thirsty soul. At that point her physical need became less important to her because she now found the true answer to her problem. Her life of disgrace was now covered by His grace love and forgiveness. She believed in Jesus to satisfy her so she will be never thirsty again. We must be willing to drink deeply again and again from the wells of salvation which Jesus offers us through His word other wise it is very easy to draw back in our hearts, or become complacent and luke warm. *Psalm 63:1-5* says "O God, thou art my God; early will I seek Thee, my flesh longeth for Thee, in a dry and thirsty land where no water is; To see Thy power and Thy glory, so as I have seen Thee in the sanctuary. Because Thy loving kindness is better than life my lips shall praise Thee. Thus will I bless Thee while I live: I will lift up my hands in Thy Name. My soul shall be satisfied as with marrow and fatness; and my mouth shall praise Thee with joyful lips." *King James Bible.* We must long for the Lord! Thirst after Him; pursue Him as our only desire. The world is thirsty and dry; so we must find our full satisfaction in Him so that His power and glory is revealed to them. Seeking Him early does not only refer to a time frame but to the fact that we must seek Him diligently before trouble strikes so we would not be found dry and thirsty. There is no water of life in the world and after our interactions with the affairs of this life whether it is our jobs, traveling and commuting and so on we do need to run to the Lord for a fresh drink of His water! We should long for Him and His loving kindness so that we can praise Him and be refreshed and renewed.

"If any man is thirsty let him come to me and drink." *John 7:37. King James Bible.*

"Wait and listen everyone who is thirsty! Come to the waters; and he who has no money, come, buy and eat! Yes, come, buy [priceless spiritual] wine and milk without money and without price [simply for the self-surrender, that accepts the blessing]." *Isaiah 55:1. AMP.Amplified Bible.* The invitation is free to all. No one needs to go on seeking to find satisfaction in relationships, drugs alcohol, sex or any other substitute.

We hear stories of people who obviously were thirsty and did not even know. The devil may have offered them alcohol or nicotine in small amounts in an effort to cause their thirst to increase so he could get them into street drugs or some other destructive habit. Satan's motive is to do all he can to ruin the future by tempting people to refuse God and sin against Him. His desire is to have their lives so twisted that they become chained to their past. Thank God that the blood of Jesus cleanses the past and wipes it clean and offers a new beginning.

"Instead of your former shame you shall have a two fold recompense. Instead of dishonor and reproach your people shall rejoice in their portion." *Isaiah 61:7. AMP. Amplified Bible.* We are therefore set free from the shame of the past. Jesus saw a woman in the synagogue one time who was bent so low that she could not lift up herself. All she could see was the ground. *Luke 13:11-13.* Jesus said to her "woman thou art loosed from thine infirmity." No one could lift up themselves on their own. Whenever you are bound in what ever area of your life one word from God can cause your life to be straightened out. When Jesus spoke, she instantly straightened up and broke out in praise. Maybe like this woman you may not be bent over physically, but emotionally bent out of shape bound by a spirit of shame which causes you to keep your head down; your mind may be afflicted and your personality is bent. Even though you are born again you cannot seem to enter into fullness of joy due to your past. The hurt, pain and weight of condemnation weighs you down. You don't have to receive the lies of the devil or a false image of yourself any more. You don't need to go to the psychic hot lines seeking answers and listening to the lies of the enemy. All you have to do is to get into the presence of God and drink deeply from the Fountain of Life until you know who you are in Christ, and you understand that you are complete in Him and you have been accepted by Him.

THE FATHER ABSENCE SYNDROME.

The desperate cry of this generation is for fathers. People want to be fathered. Fathers were intended by God the Father to be His representatives of fatherhood in the earth. The Apostle Paul said "I bow my knees before the Father of our Lord Jesus Christ, for whom every family in heaven and earth is named [that Father from whom all fatherhood takes it's title and derives it's name"] *Ephesians 3:14-15. AMP. AMPLIFIED BIBLE.*

The "man", as far as God's plan is concerned is I believe responsible for leading his family in the way of righteousness and godly living, meanwhile demonstrating to His family the Father's heart. The man was first formed and then the woman according to the account in Genesis 2. Also the scripture says *"A man is responsible to Christ, a woman is responsible to her husband, and Christ is responsible to God". 1 Corinthians 11:3. NLT. NEW LIVING TRANSLATION.* Verse 7 states that the man is the "image and [reflected] glory of God [his function of government reflects the majesty of the divine Rule]. *AMP.* The word glory means all that God has and is.

THE PROBLEM BEGAN IN THE GARDEN

From the beginning man was meant to assume the full responsibility for his wife and family. There can be no replacement for this God ordained order. Satan's first attack on the human race was not directly to the man, for he knew that Adam was given the positive command that "you may freely eat of every tree of the garden, but of the tree of the knowledge of good and evil and blessing and calamity you shall not eat, for in the day that you eat of it you shall surely die." *Genesis 2:16-17.*

So, he went to the woman instead whom he knew was the weaker vessel. He got her to question God's command and so sell out to him. Her spirit became darkened and from that point she operated in the realm of her soul. Satan knew that once this first step was accomplished she would be unable to have pure communication with Adam anymore. This was his way to move in on the human race. This carefully orchestrated plan was to cause Adam to sin which he did by partaking of the fruit from the tree which he was commanded not to touch. Having been plunged into darkness within his spirit and separated from God, Adam now had a sinful nature which has been passed down to all successive generations through the ages. The death which God warned about, which occurred as a result of disobedience occurred immediately, not in the physical realm but in the spiritual....in the spirit of Adam and Eve cutting off their communication and fellowship with God.

Now the spirit of man is where God must reside and have complete rule; the soul must yield to the spirit and the body was meant to serve not only as a house for the spirit and soul but also to serve in complete submission to the spirit. After the fall of man in the garden. This order was immediately reversed and man lived unable to hear God's voice or communicate with Him as He had planned. The spirit of man became darkened and rebellious. Even the beauty of the outward garment of light was stripped away and Adam and Eve found themselves naked and ashamed. Thank God that we who have trusted in Christ to be our Saviour and Lord will one day be clothed upon with our glorified bodies full of light and as the bible says in 1 JOHN 3:2 AS SONS AND DAUGHTERS OF GOD, we will be like Him because we shall see Him as He is.

JESUS CAME TO RESTORE GOD'S PRESENCE AND FATHERHOOD.

Jesus came to reconcile us to God; to illumine our darkness and give us new light in our spirits restoring us back to fellowship with God our heavenly Father. Every person who turns to Jesus now in faith receives cleansing and forgiveness of sins through His precious blood, and has a reborn spirit indwelt by God's Holy Spirit.

THE GENERATION CRIES OUT TO SEE THE FATHER'S HEART

As darkness continues to invade this world due to sin in various forms, there has been a complete break down in the family unit; God's order again being attacked by the enemy of all righteousness. Just as Adam abdicated his responsibilities in the garden to protect and cover his wife from the wiles of the enemy, so it is now we see men from every walk of life abandoning their homes and families.

The divorce rate being what it is has skyrocketed, leaving untold numbers of homes single parented by a mother in the majority of cases. There are times when the abandoned wife experiencing hardship, loneliness, fear and financial difficulties, turns to a substitute to fill the void in helping to father her children.

Multitudes of cases have come to light from this type of situation where the substitute father sometimes physically abuses the woman or sexually abuses the children. Worst yet there are instances where even the biological fathers do these very things. Some fathers are too busy in the business sector, searching for financial gain and social recognition following a pattern of greed. This in no way refers to fathers who are the total breadwinners for their families where couples agree to sacrifice in some way for the woman to become the home maker and so take care of her children and manage all aspects of the home. Very often some of these arrangements between couples are very stable and solid and work very successfully from what I have seen. There is no hard and fast rule where this is concerned because each home must do what is the best and smoothest workable arrangement for their families. In many other cases the woman must work or wants to work and it works just as well.

Nevertheless some fathers are physically present, yet the children feel neglected and abandoned. The deadly result is a wound to the children; to sons and daughters who are supposed to be fathered, guarded, loved and protected. Multitudes of our young people are crying out for help. Some young men don't know how to express themselves, and are broken because their fathers are not present in their lives. Almost every evil in our society and around the world traces back to homes where the man was called by God to be *"On Duty"* Having given up and neglected his authority, the doors of homes have been left wide open for the "father of lies" to enter in and so destroy the families.

It would seem as though 95% of the people in the jails today, or on the streets, on drugs or in some type of destructive lifestyle seem to say "my father left when I was too young to know him" or "I don't even know my father, he abused me, he put me down and never provided for me or cared". "My father abused my mother and my siblings and I hate him". This is the deep cry from the wounded hearts of this generation. Others may say "he was there but never thought it important to develop a relationship with me, so I never really knew him nor did he know me".

Healing has got to come to us from the Father's heart. Jesus represented the Father and brought the gift of being reconciled to God down to earth. He spoke often of God as His Father over and over again in the Gospels. "But Jesus answered them, My Father has worked [even] until now, [He has never ceased working] and I too, must be at [divine] work." I am able to do nothing from Myself [independently, of My own accord-but only as I am taught by God and as I get His orders]. Even as I hear, I judge [I decide as I am bidden to decide. As the voice comes to Me, so I give a decision], and My judgment is right [just, righteous], because I do not seek or consult My own will [I have no desire to do what is pleasing to Myself, My own aim, My own purpose] but only the will and pleasure of the Father who sent Me." JOHN 5:17.30. *AMP. Amplified Bible.* He said "if you have seen Me you have seen the Father". The Father sent Me. I do nothing of Myself but only what I see the Father do. He said the Father loves us and that we are now free to come boldly to the Father. He kept pointing us to the Father so that we know we do have a Father in heaven Who cares. He taught us to pray "our Father Who art in heaven Hallowed be Thy Name", which is the greatest prayer I believe, because in it Jesus is introducing us into a father and son relationship and into the very family of God the Father, offering us the blessed privilege to bear the family name, and giving us the assurance that we are welcome, loved and accepted. He is the Father "of whom the whole family in heaven and earth is named". *Ephesians 3:5* It speaks of endearment and security in His presence. Before Jesus came God was not referred to as a Father by the Old Testament saints. They called Him most times by the covenant names which He revealed Himself to them as; according to how He manifested Himself in various ways, as He intervened in their affairs they ascribed to Him names as Jehovah Jireh, the Lord provides, or Jehovah Tsidkenu, the Lord our righteousness, and so on. There was no way that sinful man could enter into fellowship or have a relationship with a Holy God, except through animal sacrifices which were prescribed as mandatory at that time. The Jewish leaders during the ministry of Jesus became very angry with Him for referring repeatedly to God as His Father and claimed that He was making Himself equal to God. They knew that God was holy and could not be approached except through the blood of animals and by the intervention of the high priest once a year on the Day of Atonement. So that when Jesus came they could not comprehend the truth that He was sent to become the ultimate High Priest and the one who would shed His blood to cover man's sin forever; they could not see or accept Him as the Son of God and the One who came to bring them close to God where they could know Him as their Father. They claimed to know Him and boasted that they have Him as their Father, but could not accept or put their trust in Jesus the Son as their Saviour and the One who was sent to reveal the Father's heart. "This made the Jews more determined than ever to kill Him [to do away with Him]; because He not only was breaking the Sabbath, but He actually was speaking of God as being [in a special sense] His own Father, making Himself equal [putting Himself on a level] with God." "Even the Father judges no one, for He has given all judgment [the last judgment and the whole business of judging] entirely into the hands of the Son. So that all men may give honor [reverence, homage] to the Son, just as they give honor to the Father. [In fact] whoever does not honor the Son does not honor the Father, Who has sent Him." *John 5:18,22,23. AMP. Amplified Bible.* Jesus came to reveal to us and to bring us into this wonderful relationship with our heavenly Father through His life, death and resurrection. God is a Father. He is not "the man upstairs" as some refer to Him as. This ascribes to Him a character of one who is sitting up there in a high and lofty place completely separate and distant from the lives of men. This is simply not true for the bible says "no one has ever seen God. But His only Son, who is Himself God, is near to the Father's heart; He has told us about Him." *John 1:18. NLT. New Living Translation.* "For God was in Christ, reconciling the world to Himself, no longer counting people's sins against them". *2 Corinthians 5:19. NLT. New Living Translation..* "But now in Christ Jesus, you who once were [so] far away, through [by, in] the blood of Christ have been brought near." "For it is through Him that we both whether Jew or Gentile [whether far off or near] now have an introduction [access by one [Holy] Spirit to the Father [so that we are able to approach Him]. *Ephesians 2:13,18. AMP. Amplified Bible.* Jesus has brought us back to our Father's house which is our ultimate home for all eternity. He said "I go to prepare a place for you and if I go I will come again to receive you unto Myself that where I am there you may be also." *John 1:14:3.* He prayed in His great High Priestly prayer that we would share His glory and be one with Him and with the Father. *John:17:22.* God loves us so very much and desires us to understand that He has already paved the way for us to come near to Him and not be afraid. More than being near to us He lives in us by the power of the Holy Spirit when we receive Jesus Christ as our personal Lord and Saviour and have our sins forgiven. "The Spirit of truth, Whom the world cannot receive [welcome, take to it's heart] because it does not see Him or know and recognize him. But you know and recognize Him for He lives with you [constantly] and will be in you." We have received the Spirit of adoption as sons and daughters whereby we can cry "Abba Father" Father dear Father. Jesus wants men to know and understand who the Father really is so that they can draw from Him the anointing and display His heart to this hurting generation. "For we have not received the spirit of bondage again to fear, but ye have received the Spirit of adoption, whereby we cry, Abba, Father". ROMANS 8:15. So many people are hurting both young and old. They long for someone to introduce them to what is real. Not just to hear about the God who is Omnipotent and Omnipresent, All powerful and Almighty [even though this is all true] but that He longs to be a Father to them.

Men need to arise and be able to say to our generation of young people in the way of character and anointing "if you have seen me, you have seen the

Father", by demonstrating the Father's heart. Many times most men have not yet solved the issues with their own biological fathers, so the problem seems to be grave. Could it be that many men are still carrying wounds secretly from their past due to the absence of their fathers from their lives in their growing up stages. Some people can navigate through these types of problems and emerge more or less unaffected or develop an attitude of determination to not let the circumstances which happened in their lives affect their future. In these cases they can become model fathers and husbands, making every effort to break that old cycle and not allow their own children to suffer or be affected in the way that they were. Others somehow are weaker and are not able to shake and break the cycle from their lives and so give birth to their following generation experiencing the syndrome of being unfathered.

God wants to heal these wounds, so that one generation to another may arise and praise Him. He does want there to be generations that know Him and His love for them. We must bring healing to them for many are secretly bitter and resentful. They act out of whatever they have experienced.

Nine out of ten teenage boys, girls and young adults are experiencing the absence or neglect of a father. The apostle Paul in *Ephesians 6:4* gives the admonition against embittering or wounding the children. Like I said, you could be a father physically present in your home but not in the day to day occurrences of your children's lives. For born again fathers it has to go even beyond telling them about Jesus, prattling off scripture verses by way of lectures and then forcing them to come to church, even under a threat.

Jesus said "if you had known me [had learned to recognize me] you would also have known my Father. From now on you know Him and have seen Him. Phillip said to Him, Lord show us the Father [cause us to see the Father; that is all we ask] then we shall be satisfied. Jesus replied, have I been with all of you for so long a time and do you not recognize and know me yet Phillip? Anyone who has seen me has seen the Father. How can you say then show us the Father? Do you not believe that I am in the Father and that the Father is in me? What I am telling you I do not say on my own authority and of my own accord, but the Father who lives continually in me does the works". *John 14:10. AMP Amplified Bible*

The Father lives in Jesus and Jesus lives in us by the power of the Holy Spirit. Perhaps some fathers need to take a fresh look at Jesus, in order to see the Father and understand the Father's heart. Jesus told Phillip "you have seen me you have seen the Father". There is great devastation in the world and this may increase as we get closer and closer to the coming back of Jesus for His own. The commission of the church is to arise in this hour with an anointing from the Father's heart which reaches out to the unfathered, and especially those in our churches. I say unfathered because there is a big difference between being fatherless and being unfathered. A fatherless person is one whose biological father is no longer in this earth.

In *1 John 2:14.* John writes "I write to you fathers because you have come to know [recognize, be conscious of and understand] Him who [has existed] from the beginning. I write to you young men because you are strong and vigorous, and the word of God is [always abiding in you [in your hearts] and you have been victorious over the wicked one] *Amplified Bible.* How can we see the fulfillment of this charge where our young men and women are strong, have the word of God abiding in their hearts and have victory over satan in every area, unless there are fathers raised up who know and recognize their Heavenly Father as the Father from whom all fatherhood derives it's name? Biological fathers contribute to giving physical life to their children while spiritual fathers are life giving mature believers....mature men who stand up and speak life because they know the Father of mercies and the God of all comfort. *2 Corinthians !:3.* They know that He has existed from the beginning and that He can comfort and help those in need, allowing His life and wisdom to flow through them with love and compassion to heal the wounded. So many people need to be pointed to the Father. Jesus said "I am the way the truth and the life"; no one comes to the Father except through me" *John 14:6.* People who have suffered and have been wounded in one way or another from abuse, absence or neglect of a father need to know that Jesus came to reveal the Father to them so that they could be healed. Without a deep revelation of the heart of our heavenly Father which is what Jesus came here on this earth and lived died and rose again to reveal there is not much hope for this generation.

This is the key: knowing, learning and experiencing more about the life of Jesus as revealed in the word of God. He said "if you keep my commandments [if you continue to obey my instructions] you will abide in my love and live on in it, just as I have obeyed my Father's commandments and live on in His love" *John15:10. AMP. Amplified Bible.* Jesus requires obedience, for this is the only way for the love and compassion of the Father's heart to be revealed. In concluding His High priestly prayer Jesus said to His Father " I have made your name known and revealed your character and your very self; and I will continue to make [you] known, that the love which you have bestowed upon me may be in [felt in their hearts] and that I myself may be in them" *John17:26. AMP. Amplified Bible.* Again here is the true heart of our heavenly Father revealed. Jesus makes the Father's Name known so that His love, His mercy and compassion may be felt in the hearts of His people.

His greatest commandment is *Love.* "This is my commandment that you love one another" *John15:12.* "And this is his order [his command, his injunction] that we should believe in [put our faith and trust in and adhere to and rely on] the name of his son Jesus Christ [the Messiah] and that we should love one another just as He commanded us'" *1John3:23. AMP. Amplified Bible.*

This is abiding and as we abide in Him, He becomes our home and our hearts become His home so that the Father's heart is clearly seen by all. This is where healing begins. When God gave me the revelation that He was my true Father I wept. I was on a train, and I was in the beginning stages of writing this book. All of a sudden the Holy Spirit impressed this so clearly upon my heart, and almost immediately I felt something lift from my heart. A heaviness left me and I felt such a release. He showed me that He was the Father that I was always longing for and that I did not need any more substitutes. From that time the words on my lips have constantly been *"Father".* It feels so wonderful to be certain that He is my heavenly Father and that He cares so much. Now I do have and forever will have the abounding assurance that He is my Father. This makes me so very happy. I did at the time know a little about what the Word of God said about Him being a Father but I was so blinded by pain and unbelief that I never experienced this truth until that time. Now I am very secure and strong with a definite sense of belonging because I do know He loves me and will never leave me. Everyone needs this understanding. God works in various ways; this was how He chose to reveal himself to me as my Father. He will also reveal Himself to everyone who is hurting and unable to feel whole because of that most important missing person in their lives! Their fathers!

You see being male does not make you a father. Having a baby does not do it. In the age which we now live teenage boys are becoming "fathers" and they have no idea of what this really means! They are really boys and need to mature into true manhood which really could only happen as a result of their coming to know the plan of God for their lives. It is a fact also that there are many wonderful fathers ; people who never accepted Christ as their Lord and Saviour out there, who know what it is to provide, nurture, and care for their children, love them and be there for them. But this does not and cannot negate the truth of the need for spiritual fathers who know the Father's heart, who are growing in grace and producing the fruit of the Spirit, to lead many into the ways of righteousness and mentor them into the things of God as He has planned. This is really Christ likeness and I believe is maturity for every child of God. Many of our young people really want to serve God and to know Him; most of them in the natural are wounded from abandonment and neglect of their fathers and even though they have received Jesus they seem not to be able to progress in their walk and growth in Him because they still need to know the touch of the Father. This is not an isolated occurrence to the young alone but happens even to several adults, who have not been able to understand Him as not being the human father whom they had known. He is love and love never fails! The weaknesses and failings of those who were responsible to shape our lives for our futures cannot be attached or ascribed to Him. It becomes so very difficult to so many people to be able to relate to God as a Father. Due to their past experiences, and the influences of circumstances which have shaped their personalities and lives they transfer whatever their natural fathers did or did not do to God the Father. You see no one has seen God at any time and the God that most people see is reflected in and through those who are in authority over us. Whatever environment existed in the home as many grew up with their human fathers, causes thoughts, ideas and concepts of God the Father to be much distorted. If human fathers were unkind, brutal or weak willed people, full of sarcasm and just plain unloving, these negative impressions and memories go a long way and are very damaging. Very often many are so wounded by these human failures and frailties of their biological fathers that it is difficult for them to see God the heavenly Father any other way. It takes some people a very long time to really understand the loving heart of our Heavenly Father and to realize that He in no way should be compared or ascribed the character of the human father in negative ways. They judge Him as one who cannot be trusted and who really does not care too much about human suffering. They know that their sins have been forgiven and pardoned through Jesus Christ, but have great difficulty due to past memories to go on to the next stage of being victorious over satan in all areas. This is like the fork in the road for many. The pain is unbearable and their questions are unanswered. I believe it is worst sometimes for men than for women in some cases but altogether in general we all hurt. Imagine going through most of your entire life trying to navigate through this world in it's present state with this type of pain. Whatever foundation you have had, determines what you would manifest. For those who have heard others talk about their fathers and the wonderful relationship they enjoy with them, and know that they have to be silent during such conversations causes some to be really ashamed. If this cycle continues it would produce nothing but hurting wounded people in need of restoration. But the good news is that this is the very thing that Jesus came to do. Restore broken wounded people to the Father's love. God has provided a healing balm for this generation and is calling on many of us to take the place in the positions he has for us so that He could release His healing through their lives to heal the broken hearted. Jesus came to heal the broken hearted and to bind up the wounds. This is the Father's will.

It is not enough for people to be in church and still never attain to wholeness. Some people can be lost right in the church. They hide behind coverings and when this is not rightly discerned the results can be devastating.

There are some who once loved the presence of God and have known to worship but have taken off and retreated in disappointment and hurt. Why? They have yet to experience the Father's heart. They want something genuine and real. They want to know that there is someone whom they can trust and someone who loves them, and can introduce them to the security which they long for. People are in search of the authentic. They know the real from the phony and they sometimes get trapped and deceived with what the world offers in the way of "keeping things real". They may not be able to explain exactly what they are looking for but they are looking for something to fill the voids in their hearts.

There are young men everywhere and even in our churches needing godly mature men to call forth their masculinity because they have been injured by the absence of their fathers. Young women also are suffering and confused ending up making the wrong choices because their fathers were also absent or neglectful. Biological fathers should know how to embrace their daughters even while they are very young in a pure sense which helps them to know they are loved and secured by the strength of their fathers' touch. So should our young men also experience the embrace of their fathers so they are affirmed in their masculine roles for the future. Many do have the blessing of this experience, but the percentage of those who know nothing of this type of pure communication with their fathers far out weighs it. Most fathers want to shake hands with their sons from even an early age, thinking that they are introducing them to the world of manhood. Crying is sometimes interrupted by such words as "big boys do not cry; stand up and be a man"! This makes some think that they are doing the right thing but when literal tears are withheld, they can become so hardened inside from repeatedly hearing that type of message that while it sounds good, it never silences the true need for affection and genuine love. The result more often than ever is their resorting to the bed of immorality looking for affection in all the wrong places! They are really hungry for affection but if they never received this from their own parents it becomes difficult for them in turn to interact with their own children most times. Whatever foundation you have had will determine what fruit you manifest and how it affects the lives of those in your specific sphere of influence.

TAKING THE POSITION WHICH GOD INTENDED

Drawing close to Jesus will cause us to discern the cry of this generation, and also to hear the voice of the shepherd who wants to lead them back to the Fatherhood of God. Young men need mature godly men to sit them down and discuss with them about future everyday issues, about money management, education, success, dating, marriage and sex, all based on biblical truths. They need to know that God is their father, and as they surrender their lives to Him they are accepted in Jesus the beloved, *Ephesians 1:6.* He is concerned about each little detail of their lives just as He cares for the sparrows *Luke12:6.* I am talking about speaking God's word and promises over the lives of wounded broken people in wisdom, faith, authority and love, so that they may be restored and rise up in the power of the Holy Spirit to do exploits for God.

We do need to see so many more godly men rise up to this challenge and accept responsibility so that we can see a move of God unlike anything we have ever seen in any generation. We need to pray for the spirit of Elijah to be released in many of the men of this generation to reconcile the hearts of the estranged fathers to the ungodly children, and the hearts of the rebellious children to the piety of their fathers. *Malachi 4:6.* Remembering that wherever there is Elijah there is an Elisha waiting to receive the mantle. It is about mentoring and being examples to the next generation as God intended so that they know the Father and understand His love, calling, and are confirmed in their respective roles of walking out God's plan and will for their lives. That they fully understand what it means to be saved and can set their hope on God fully.

This is so very much needed especially in homes where single parents are having such a hard time in raising their children. We do not need nor is it the will of the father for the world to teach our children.

There are several people who speak negatively over the young, continually and are expecting to see situations change in their lives. This is not the will of God nor is it His heart. Life and death is in the power of the tongue, and many need to repent for the use of their tongues concerning young people and ask the Father to cancel the power of those words. We should all be obedient to God now and speak life as He has commanded us to for we shall all give an account for every idle and non-productive word which we speak.

Some young men are hiding behind wounds; being busy with jobs, trying to "make something of their lives" or even fitting in with religious duties and sports! This of course helps them to avoid the issues which are painful. Others are disrespectful to women and many others enter into identity confusion. In the bondage of self preservation and fear caged in by anger, they need to know that they do not have to hide within the prison of themselves but can receive the Father's love.

For those who have grown into physical manhood but are still griping and mourning for their fathers, unable to experience wholeness, you need to forgive your earthly fathers, whether they are dead or alive or even if you have never seen them! You see the bible says there is a time to mourn and grieve, and a time to stop grieving and laugh! Weeping may endure for a night but joy comes in the morning. It is necessary to grieve over the pain of the situation; even lament over it for some time for this is healthy to our overcoming the past emotional wounding. It is not wise when wronged to deny it. It is healthy to admit that a wrong was inflicted without allowing ourselves to remain in the grip or bond of bitterness and revenge. Revenge does not contribute to anyone's healing. As a matter of fact revenge leads to hate and hate is most destructive. Trying to seek for answers from God may only prolong the healing process because He is not obliged to answer us for every thing we encounter here in this life. Even if He does, this does not necessarily cause the pain to subside away from us. Vengeance belongs to God alone and so we ought not to put ourselves in His place by taking our own stand in the matter either. We ought not to build our altars there and pitch our tents in that same place for the rest of our natural lives. We can learn real life lessons from people like Joseph the son of Jacob in the book of Genesis, who was so badly mistreated by his very own brothers. After a series of circumstances in the divine providence of God, he met with his brothers, and after weeping uncontrollably faced the pain of the situation with a heart of forgiveness and said "what was done was meant for evil, *but God* turned it for good so that many lives would be saved". He refused to be judgemental, seek revenge or stand in the place of the Almighty God.   There is a dying world out there that needs to know that we have been where they are, and the only way to hope and restoration is through Jesus Christ the Son of the living God. When Elijah after a great demonstration of the power of God ran helplessly in fear of the threat which Jezebel unleashed on him, he ran into a cave; but the Spirit of the Lord met him there and asked "What are you doing here?" he tearfully mourned his complaint of the sin of the children of Israel and said that he was the only one who was left alone. He even said that he was no better than his forefathers. This of course was not completely true for God who knows all things informed him that there were 7000 more who did not bow to the foreign god or kissed the lips of the idol. He was called out of the cave and given instructions in his fearful state to go on to do the Lord's business, and carry out His commission of transferring the anointing to those God had made ready to carry out His service. *1Kings 19:9-15.* God is calling many to come out of the caves of despair and mourning, self pity and fear to carry out His great commission of winning the lost confused generation at any cost.

Forgive the forefathers for whatever they have done to harm you. Surrender your whole heart to Jesus and if need be seek godly counsel from those anointed with the Spirit of God to reveal the Father's heart. Also realize that your own father may not have had the privilege to be lovingly fathered either and so had not been able to be a father to you. No one can give what they do not have or have never received. This process of forgiveness must be worked out in the daughters also who are hurting and wounded because of what their fathers did or did not do. God is calling on us who would hear His voice now and who are willing to move forward to release the mistakes of our fathers and even mothers in some cases in forgiveness and enter into newness of life so that you could help other hurting people. "So take a new grip with your tired hands and stand firm on your shaky legs. Mark out a straight path for your feet. Then those who follow you, though they are weak and lame will not stumble and fall but will become strong." *Hebrews12:12-13. New Living Translation.*

Holding on to the past hurts and sins of your parents will only keep you bound and hinder you from receiving any deliverance. God wants you free and has provided a way but you must be willing to forgive. He knows how to deal with sin and His way is for us to release the wrong doer. He said vengeance is His and he would repay and recompense. God is calling you out from the bondage of the past; calling you forth from your father's house, and even from your mother's house if you have suffered from the failings and negative character designs of both parents: [from the sins, short comings transgressions and bonds] in your mind and emotions to a much higher calling. If you will respond then you will see Him for who He is and you will most certainly cry *Aba Father*! You must forgive so that you can be forgiven and that your prayers will be heard. *Mark11:24-25.* We can emulate the characteristics of our forefathers only if they left behind them a legacy for us of the fear and love for the Lord Jesus Christ, and proved by their lives in word and deed that they lived in the love and grace of God, upholding the word of God and had a great honor for the blood of Jesus and the Name of Jesus. If we know for a fact that these qualities were not true of them, while we love and respect them as we ought to, we must endeavor to not carry on the traits and sinful lives that they may have lived in ignorance and lack of understanding of God. As a generation we have been entrusted with a wealth of wisdom knowledge and understanding of God, maybe more than any generation, and we are highly accountable to Almighty God for what we do with it. We are entrusted with the revelation of the love of God, walking in the Spirit and so much more. We must be so grateful to our Father for all He has given to us in His mercy and determine to walk and live lives that show forth who He is in us through Jesus Christ. We cannot repeat the same mistakes and sins of the forefathers, knowing that they did not leave a worthy benediction when they departed.

GOD HAS A SPECIAL PLACE FOR WOMEN

Women also have a part to play in giving birth to this great move of God. "Thus saith the Lord of Hosts, consider ye, and call for the mourning women that they may come; and send for cunning women, that they may come and let them make haste and take up a wailing for us that our eyes may run down with tears and our eye lids gush out with waters" *Jeremiah 9:17-18.* Women to cry out to God for the men; for the vision of God to be birthed in their hearts so they can be so surrendered. I must say that as women God has created us in such a unique way with an ability to conceive and to give birth both naturally and spiritually. We have been given the sensitivity to feel as it were, to groan with the pains of childbirth over all types of situations which we face in our personal lives and in the lives of those we come in contact with. We must never allow the world to harden us or mould us into it's teaching to be tough or competitive with men. God has designed us in this way so that we feel the pains of situations and of the hurting generation and so through our intercession we give birth to great things in the kingdom of God. I believe that it is a ministry that God wants us to enter into and take very seriously. "for as soon as Zion travailed , she brought forth her children". *Isaiah 66:8.* There were women selected in Jeremiah's time to wail and mourn over the situations taking place and to prepare the way for God to intervene.

It cannot please God when our sons and daughters turn to the world looking for answers; when satan offers them a false restoration, false identity and deception! God cannot be glorified when sons and daughters are in jail, pursued by a run away spirit, on drugs, active in immorality or threatening suicide. This is not supposed to be in the family of the redeemed or accepted as the normal thing for us, but it happens all the time. "Thy sons and thy daughters shall be given unto another people, and thine eyes shall look and fail with longing for them all the day long: and there shall be no might in thine hand. *Deuteronomy28:32.* Now we are redeemed from this because "Christ purchased our freedom [redeeming us] from the curse [doom] of the law [and it's condemnation] by Himself becoming a curse for us, for it is written [in the scriptures] cursed is every one who hangs on a tree [is crucified]". *Galatians 3:13. AMP. Amplified Bible.* God sent Jesus to bless us and our families, and even though satan desires to have our children and pursues a well devised plan to carry this through, we must stand against this in the power of the Holy Spirit commanding him to release our sons and daughters. It is a fight but it is a good fight, for sons and daughters are the property of the Father. We must continue to stand, for God said having done all to stand, He did not say how long we were to stand for. Just stand. So we can claim that our children shall not be given into captivity or to another people and be claimed by the spirit of the world, but shall serve the true and the living God who gave His Son for them. God gave His Son so that He might bring many sons and daughters into glory!

As older mature women some of us can and should speak life, as well as through prayer and intercession we could offer godly examples and do our part to help the upcoming daughters in the Body of Christ to know the Lord better. I don't think that you have to be a biological mother to stand in the gap and bring hope and restoration to a hurting young woman or young girl, or to any one for that matter. As women destined by God to conceive, God can put a burden in the womb of our spirit for some hurting teen or young woman and by the sensitivity of the Holy Spirit we can begin to pray and call on God for captives to be set free, and also aid in the nurturing process. God is calling many of us to get into the birthing position and He is also calling for the spiritual midwives to get ready to receive the new born babies in love as He clothes them in their garments of righteousness. We are uniquely called to help nurture the younger women, and to pray for them until Christ is truly formed in them.

BREAK THE CYCLE OF EVIL.

I declare that it is time to break the generational curse cycle which satan has master minded: the curse of fatherlessness. This is God's plan for the generations of His people: "for He established a testimony [an express precept] in Jacob and appointed a law in Israel, commanding our fathers that they should make [the great facts of God's dealings with Israel] known to their children, that the generation to come might know them, that the children still to be born might arise and recount them to their children. That they might set their hope in God and not forget the works of God but might keep His commandments and not be as their fathers- a stubborn and rebellious generation that set not their hearts to know God, and whose spirits were not steadfast and faithful to God". *Psalm 78:5-7. AMP. Amplified Bible.*

In order for the upcoming present generation and the generation to come to experience God, he is commissioning those who would hear His voice to begin to make Him known to them. Holding on to the sins and rebellion of the past generations regardless of whether they sinned against you personally through abuse of whatever kind will stop the flow of the Father's love from being revealed. We will have nothing to offer them but the woes and sorrows of the past which brings in hopelessness. God wants them to set their hope in Him. Jesus said "and this is eternal life: [it means] to know [to perceive, recognize, become acquainted with and understand You the only true and real God and likewise to know Jesus as the Christ [the Anointed One the Messiah] Whom You have sent. *John 17:3. AMP. Amplified Blble.* The prayer is for the wind of the Spirit to blow profusely over a hurting wounded people bringing healing and wholeness to all ages. We have to determine to understand the tremendous responsibility given to us in this present generation to sever all ties and renounce all practices of the past generations who did not commit their lives to the Lord Jesus Christ, and make radical decisions not to go in such directions. The reason being that we being now enlightened, are highly accountable to God for all the truths which we receive as the end of the ages draws near. We are in a better position than past generations because there is so much more exposure to the light of God's word now and much more intensity of preaching and teaching and a wide assortment of technology available as the return of Jesus draws near. We do not live just unto ourselves, but everything we do or say results in a seed sown which will affect the generation after us either negatively or positively.

SEARCHING FOR REALITY

A young man or woman can suppress pain until it turns into anger and hate. In that state they search for identity and can become filled with deception. Then they turn to the world for the answers. Here the enemy of the family unit ushers them into the world's pattern as a cure and answer which promises a counterfeit relief.

Gangs are formed by those who have rebelled against all authority and bought the lie and false perception of love. They look for a sense of belonging, and unable to find this in their homes for various reasons, they retreat outside to the streets where destruction is inevitable unless God intervenes. They claim to love each other, care for each other and be loyal to each other but resort to violence, murder and blood shed. They obviously have a distorted view of the Father and His love for them. What satan is after all the time is the complete destruction of the family unit and order which God established.

Gang members are brought together by satan to form a sort of "family." One of them assumes the leadership role and controls all the others in the name of "love." They claim not to have any experience of their father's love or involvement in their lives and sometimes blame both parents. The leader actually thinks he is a "father" and initiates the discipline for the followers, puts them in fear, for this is the ruling device of satan's kingdom while devising organized plans to do harm to others.

The "gay" community on the other hand have been blinded and deceived in their search to find true identity and belonging. They have been drawn into same sex relationships which promise them pleasure, comfort and happiness, but cannot satisfy the deep longing and desires for wholeness or heal the pain and wound which they have experienced somewhere in their lives. The relief is only temporary and leads to despair. In their sexual brokenness they run towards a false promise of freedom, pride, sympathy, understanding and compassion. They have sought refuge in this type of behavior because they responded to feelings which led them to accept a false identity and false image of themselves as well as a false concept of the Fatherhood of God.

They blame Him and accuse parents for their feelings. Many of them need to experience the Father's love and forgiveness, so they can forgive those who have wronged them knowingly or unknowingly. Not all of them have turned their backs on God for there are many who would like us to hear their stories and desire to be rescued. We do know that the adversary does not give up without a fight but the greater one lives in us and through our intercession and love many can be pulled out of the fire. Sometimes a parent may not even be aware that they may have offended their child. They did all they could do in the best way they knew how, but still the children are upset. [I believe that we must understand that we are not all made up the same way, and very often what may not affect one child will certainly affect another. Each one has a different emotional system and some children are prone to be more sensitive than others. Some can sail through the turbulence and high tide of any adverse situation and still emerge with an attitude and strength of a warrior and an ability to overcome all obstacles. Others are very sensitive and usually the sensitive ones are the ones who process things deeply and end up terribly scarred.]

I heard of a case where the father of a teenager constantly beat the mother. Their only child a daughter watched on helplessly as she grew up in this atmosphere. Eventually this couple separated, leaving the daughter with the mother. As the mother in loneliness most likely sought companionship, the situation degenerated into an utter fiasco resulting in the daughter hating the father and wanting to be away from the mother's life of confusion. The mother obviously thought that she was doing her best and that she needed comfort for the trouble she went through. She may also have felt that her daughter needed a father "figure". Obviously that was not the way of wisdom. Nevertheless such can find hope in the restoring power of the blood of Jesus Christ. A person who is not whole in themselves will be led to attract the wrong relationships or seek help from the arm of flesh.

Sometimes parents' actions can be misunderstood and our children receive it as an injury to them. They do not want to discuss it or address it but most times suppress it and bury it while responding in ways which lead to sinful reactions such as rebellion, disrespect, and other negative behavior patterns.

Another case comes to mind of a young woman I know who shared with me a story of her parents. I met her in a work place environment when she told me this story. Realizing her tough attitude and outer appearance, I simply told her that I was doing a little survey on fathers and asked her what was her relationship like with her dad. She immediately opened up her heart to me telling me of a simple situation in her younger years which unfolded into a crisis for her entire life! When she was just a little girl she took a gallon bottle of milk out of the refrigerator and put it to her mouth to drink some of it. Some of the milk spilled on the floor [obviously because she was just a small child and could not control the contents of the bottle properly]. Her mother proceeded to tell her father who in turn punished her so severely. She was placed to kneel on the floor and so hold two heavy weights one in each hand for countless hours. Several beatings followed and other forms of abuse. This girl turned into a woman who became extremely hateful of her parents and very confused. She developed a very tough personality which manifested in actions denoting "no one will ever hurt me like this again." When she shared this story with me she was already blaming God. I had such a wonderful opportunity to share God's love with her, and to tell her that He is such a loving Father. I told her that her father may not have realized what he did and the fact that it would scar and affect her for such a long time in her life. I also mentioned to her that he too may have been abused and mistreated as a child and may not have known the love of his father. Abuse cannot be covered because it will come out in some negative way most times in the life of the abused as well as the abuser.

Whether physical, mental, emotional or verbal these patterns and traits very often [not always] can filter down into a family for generations. Not because you were abused should you go forth and abuse your children. This actually perpetuates a generational curse but Christ came to redeem us from every curse so that the blessings of wholeness can be in our families with joy and peace. No one has to say "the fathers have eaten sour grapes and the children's teeth are set on edge". *Ezekiel 18:2* because Jesus has already taken care of every sin, transgression, iniquity, emotional wound, pain or tormenting situations from past generations and for all generations to come. He has established a New Covenant through His blood and opened up a wonderful way for us to enjoy newness of life. He said …."*it is finished*"

ARE YOU A PRODIGAL?

When we look at the story of the prodigal we see attributes of God's character, His divine grace, mercy, unconditional love and long suffering, and even His ability to restore. It also reveals the heart of the Father and the fact that our salvation is not of works but by faith and trust in God's forgiveness through Jesus Christ. We see the consequences for sin and the beauty of restoration.

The word prodigal really means reckless and wasteful. Backsliding does not just happen. It begins slowly in the heart. As the individual constantly submits a little at a time to the enemy's lies and temptation, rebellion sets in. When you hold conversations and reasoning in your mind with the devil he will eventually shape your thinking and your emotions will move you into a direction to disobey God. We are told in the book of proverbs to "guard your heart with all diligence for out of it are the issues of life". *Proverbs 4:23*. Also we must gird up the loins of our minds and be sober because the devil like a roaring lion is moving around.

The moment you start to compromise your Christian standards and your walk with the Lord you have already entered into a backslidden state! The world has it's own ungodly mould, and the spirit of evil that influences it is determined to grab every human being in an effort to shape them into it's pattern. The evil influence of this world can be seen in every sector of life. The radio, the television, in the schools, colleges and every where you could think about; even in the home. That spirit is in the culture and fabric of the nations and beckons many to partake. Sad to say that there are several of God's children [and not only the young] are falling prey to the evil of this present age. It has even crept into some churches and overtaken many.

COMPROMISING YOUR STANDARDS

Suddenly you hear that person who was once on fire for God and who lived a consecrated life saying "there is nothing wrong with certain types of music, television shows, movies or other worldly activities. Such people should be on guard because these are the beginning steps down to the pig pen if you do not stop.

"And He [Jesus] said, there was a certain man who had two sons; And the younger of them said to his father, "Father, give me the part of the property that falls [to me]. And he divided the estate between them. And not many days after that the younger son gathered up all that he had and journeyed into a distant country and there he wasted his fortune on reckless and loose [from restraint] living. And when he had spent all he had, a mighty famine came upon that country, and he began to fall behind and be in want. So he went and forced [glued] himself upon one of the citizens of that country, who sent him into his fields to feed hogs. And he would gladly have fed on and filled his belly with the carob pods that the hogs were eating, but [they could not satisfy his hunger and] nobody gave him anything [better]. Then when he came to himself he said, "how many hired servants of my father have enough food, and [even food] to spare, but I am perishing [dying] here of hunger! I will get up and go to my father and will say to him, father I have sinned against heaven and in your sight. I am no longer worthy to be called your son; [just] make me like one of your hired servants." So he got up and came to his own father, but while he was still a long way off, his father saw him and was moved with pity and tenderness [for him; and he ran and embraced him and kissed him [fervently]. And the son said to him, "father I have sinned against heaven and in your sight. I am no longer worthy to be called your son. [I no longer deserve to be recognized as a son of yours]!" But the father said to his bond servants; 'bring quickly the best robe [the festive robe of honor and put it on him, and give him a ring for his hand and sandals for his feet. And bring out that [wheat] fattened calf and kill it, and let us revel and feast and be happy and make merry. Because this, my son was dead and is alive again; he was lost and is found! And they began to revel and feast and make merry." *Luke 15:11-24. AMP. Amplified Bible.*

It appears that this prodigal son had these thoughts in mind long before making a demand for his portion of the inheritance and then leaving. The father did not seem surprised or shocked at this behavior and did not seek to restrain or persuade him to remain in the house, for there may have been some "tell tale" signs of rebellion from the son as he moved around the house before deciding to leave eventually.

When you enter into prodigal living, you walk out of the light, because God is light and in Him is no darkness at all; you move out into a place which He never designed for you. We must all understand that the God whom we serve has created us to be free will moral agents, and He will not stop us if we make such decisions. Here we see the prodigal making his own choice! The bible says "let no man say when he is tempted that he is tempted of God, for

God cannot be tempted with evil neither does He tempt any man. But every man is tempted when he is drawn away of his own lust and enticed. Then when lust has conceived it bringeth forth sin: and sin when it is finished, bringeth forth death." *James 1:13-15.*

You see God will not stop you and you cannot be deceived into thinking that He is the one who is responsible for your sin and the consequences. You write your own prophesies concerning your future, and by your actions bring them to pass contrary to the will of God for your life as revealed in His word.

It is quite obvious that this boy knew right from wrong, was raised in a home that held high moral values, and he knew the good life, but somehow other things entered his heart and he wanted to leave. The lust of the outside world overwhelmed him so he wanted his entire inheritance so he could blow it in riotous ways. He never foresaw a famine down the road.

The famine begins when the euphoria is over. The so called "bright lights" of the party and the "city life" suddenly go dim and darkness sets in. This happens to everyone who enters into prodigal living.

When that which you felt was so important......which you desired your flesh to fulfill moves you to make a choice to leave the house, eventually the famine will begin. You will begin to be in want; in want of peace; in want of joy; in want of God's presence which you left and traded for riotous living; in want of fellow brothers and sisters in the Body of Christ; in want of your family whose way you decided was wrong, in want of restoration and forgiveness.

You see the world's supply will come to an end sooner or later. While you are in the house your inheritance is protected and preserved by the Father, for the Lord has promised to be our shepherd and ensures that we shall not want. When you take your inheritance to the world, the spirit of the world will steal all you've got. King Solomon warns in the book of proverbs chapter 5:9-14. "Lest thou give thine honor unto others and thy years unto the cruel; lest strangers be filled with thy wealth; and thy labors be in the house of a stranger; and thou mourn at the last, when thy flesh and thy body are consumed and say how have I hated instruction, and my heart despised reproof; and have not obeyed the voice of my teachers, nor inclined mine ear to them that instructed me! I was almost in all evil in the midst of the congregation and assembly." KING JAMES BIBLE.

For anyone who thinks that this is just another story in the Bible, this happens time and time again. There is an all out war for souls, and the enemy satan is very subtle. He is not all powerful but he does have some power. He also has a host of demons employed and ready to carry out his assignments as he sees fit and is given an opportunity. Any doors left open to him gives him free access to our lives. While you are in the house he will always seek ways to get you out. He can hardly destroy you while you are in the house…..while you are praising God, worshipping and serving Him. He will attack you and do all he can to tempt you but he cannot destroy you! Satan will use every strategy he knows to tempt you with suggestions again and again in an effort to weaken your defenses. His motive is to have you give him your attention, agree with him and then yield up your will. He does this in various ways.

As I said before the steps down to degeneration begin in your heart when you refuse to guard that precious commodity. The way to your heart is through your eyes and ears. When you begin to listen to conversations and music which are of an ungodly nature and watch television shows and movies, and read books which you know are not of God you are already headed for trouble. When you go places knowingly to be inappropriate. You bow a little at a time hoping you could stop on your own not realizing you are already trapped into satan's web.

We encounter evil every day on the streets, in the work place and the school systems. But when we listen to and tap into conversations music and literature setting our mouths to confirm and acknowledge what satan is leading us into as good and right, deception moves in and the next step is to partake of all that we have allowed into our hearts. Be sure then that you are headed down hill into the pigpen towards destruction unless you wake up and turn in repentance.

So many people are signing a "peace treaty" with the enemy as it were. Agreeing with him and his suggestions; giving what he says in temptation a place in our hearts will eventually make room for an idol to be set up. This happens when we do not give that place to God and His Word. Not long after that you will act on what you allowed in your heart, because it becomes more important to you than the Lord.

A word of warning to the parents of teenagers. You must be observant for these signs and not wait for the final shock. Like I mentioned earlier the father of the prodigal did not seem shocked at all at the boy's decision because he must have observed some signs before. We should be looking for such things as the choice of friends the teen goes around with; the music, the television shows they show interest in, their commitment to Jesus, whether they show lack of interest in ministry or maybe they are in rebellion towards you as a parent. There is hardly a parent who really loves the Lord who sits back passively while children are taking steps down to the pigpen, but very often when we plead, beg, and try to reason with them showing them their ways of error, sometimes if not more than often the only valuable lessons which our children learn are sad to say the consequences of the pigpen.

In the pigpen no one will give you anything. What you craved for ends up in unfullfilment and could even lead to death if not for the mercy and grace of God through loving intercession of Christian parents and loved ones. Condemnation is the result because you chose to walk after the law of sin and death as opposed to the law of the spirit of life in Christ Jesus. Life and death are set before us every day and we are asked to choose life so that we and our generations may live and serve the Lord. *Deuteronomy 30:19.*

Why would some of us run from such a loving Father only to end up in the pigpen of sin. We run away from Him and refuse to receive His correction and discipline while we are in the house. But the cries from the pigpen are very real. They may go something like this......"why didn't I listen; if I had only known it would be like this; I should have paid attention to God's warning when He spoke to me through my pastor and youth leader; I should have prayed before making this decision; my mother warned me but I refused to listen.

That boy did not just decide to go back to his father! He must have had his season of crying and moaning while he ate hog's food and continued to be in want. Even the one he joined himself to refused to give him anything. Ending up in the pigpen by your own choice could never be a time of comfort for any child of God. You are not a pig, but a lamb, a sheep. The mercy of God will visit you there; the hand of God will reach for you there; the intercession of the saints and loved ones will be ascending before the throne and you will come to your senses in one way or another. God let you have your way because you craved the kingdoms of the world offered by satan instead of the exceeding riches of His glorious inheritance. *Ephesians 1:18.* Satan offered you his counterfeit dreams [because he has no inheritance] and promises and you fell for it in deception, because you did not delight yourself in the Lord as you should. Choosing not to drink deeply of His Spirit and His presence in fellowship and receive His love and instruction. God has called us into fellowship with his Son Jesus Christ. When you leave His fellowship you begin to fellowship with the unfruitful works of darkness which we are told to have nothing to do with but to reprove them. *Ephesians 5:11.*

Child of God where can you go that He will not keep reaching for you to draw you back so that you will recover yourself from the snare of the devil? The psalmist asks :"whither shall I go from thy Spirit? Or whither shall I flee from thy presence? If I ascend up into heaven thou art there; if I make my bed in hell behold thou art there. Even there shall thy hand lead me and thy right hand shall hold me. If I say, surely the darkness shall cover me even the night shall be light about me." *Psalms 139:7-11.*

The prodigal went to a far country. You see from the story that no matter how far we go we could not go too far that God's hand cannot reach for us.

I would like to help some young person to understand that God loves you. Young person, Jesus loves you and has given you eternal life once you have received Him as your Lord and Saviour. You are redeemed by the blood of the Lamb of God slain from the foundation of the world. Why would you accept the things that accompany death and not the things that accompany salvation? You may be toying around with ungodliness and uncleaness and making light of it; with one foot in the world and the other in God's Presence. You cannot continue like this, because if you don't repent and receive forgiveness you will find yourself taking those dangerous steps down which lead to the pigpen. You need to keep some short accounts with God beginning right now. Your very life depends on this. *2 Corinthians 7:1.* says "having therefore these promises dearly beloved, let us cleanse ourselves from all filthiness of the flesh and spirit perfecting holiness in the fear of the Lord".

THE SPIRIT OF NEBUCHADNEZER

The spirit of Nebuchadnezer is very much alive in this hour. You see satan is the god of this world and the prince of the power of the air. His evil influence is seen and realized everywhere in the world. Many youth and several adults are being brought into bondage daily by the use of the internet for ungodly purposes.

In the Old Testament there were three Hebrew boys who were among those sent into captivity into Babylon. At that time King Nebuchadnezer made an image of gold and a commandment went out to the effect that every one who heard the sound of the flute, harp, cornet, sackbut, psaltery and all kinds of music must fall down and worship the image which was made. Any one who did not worship this idol was to be thrown into the burning fiery furnace. The three Hebrew boys, Shadrac, Meshach, and Abednego, knew the true and living God and knew that He was the only one worthy to be worshipped and adored. Even in the land of the enemy they remembered God's commandments taught to them by their forefathers. They refused to bow and were thrown into the burning fiery furnace. In the sight of the king and all others they were thrown there to perish! They fell down bound in the fire; but the king's mind became confused and astonished when he observed "did we not cast three men bound into the fire?" They answered and said to the king "true, O king". He answered and said "lo I see four men loosed, and walking in the midst of the fire and they have no hurt, and the form of the fourth is like the Son of God"! *Daniel 3.* God came to the rescue of these young men as they decided to honor Him and not bow down to the evil command. So many people are bowing down and conceding to satan's request for worship. Idolatry is at an all time high, as people are putting fleshly things into their lives in the place of God. Some are bowing to music with all kinds of ungodly demonic lyrics. Satan desires worship and will take it any way he can.

The fact is that God has made provision for us to live as over comers in this present evil society. Just as He was with those three Hebrew boys who lived in Babylon in a culture filled with evil 'greater is he who is in you than he who is in the world." *1 John 4:4*. Jesus prayed that we would not be taken out of the world but that we would be delivered from the evil one. *John 17:15*. This is a time when good is called evil and evil is exalted as good.

THE CHURCH.....GOD'S HEALING CENTER.

The steps that lead down can happen very quickly, but you don't have to assume the position of "I've fallen down and I can't get up; I can't help myself". You may not be able to help yourself in your own strength but you can call on God and He will help you to get up and He will receive you back with open arms. He will be right there waiting lovingly for you. We are told to draw near to God and He will draw near to us. Notice in the natural, when you are going to really fall, you may have tripped or missed your step, and your body may move swiftly and uncontrollably to the ground. Injury results most times; sometimes minor, sometimes major. But help is always available. Our heavenly Father has all the resources available to help us. The church is the hospital and healing center of the Body of Christ. In His body dwells the fullness of Him who fills all things with Himself. *Ephesians 1:23*. We should never make the mistake that some people do in the natural by refusing medical help made available to them. All the anointing resides in the body of Christ. All the healing, peace, forgiveness of sins, deliverance and whatever you need. It all flows from the Head of the Church, Jesus Christ our Lord and Saviour. While the offer of forgiveness holds sure we should always run to Him quickly.

"Seek ye the Lord while He may be found, call ye upon Him while He is near: let the wicked forsake his way and the unrighteous man his thoughts; and let him return unto the Lord and He will have mercy upon him and to our God and he will abundantly pardon". *Isaiah 55:6-7*.

THE MERCY OF GOD.

God is always trying to get us to turn back to Him because He wants to do us good. He is a loving and merciful Father.

The bible says concerning the prodigal then when he came to himself he said, "how many hired servants of my father have enough food and [even food] to spare, but I am perishing [dying] here of hunger". It takes a decision on our part, an act of our own will to arise from the pigpen of sin and move towards God. The world is a waterless dungeon and those who belong to it are perishing from hunger and thirst. God never moves from His position of loving us. We are always the ones who move and run away from Him.

The boy remembered his time in the house. He remembered the love peace and joy he experienced in his father's presence, and even the servants who were receiving their fill.

CROSSING LINES

Small steps off the path of righteousness, will eventually lead down to the pigpen. People who try to get too close to the line eventually end up crossing that very line. Those who reason concerning things like relationships and know what God's will is concerning dating a non christian partner or even the code of conduct while dating [in issues which the bible is very clear on still end up struggling in areas of purity, with thoughts of how far they should go in a relationship without crossing lines. Compromise is the order of the day and always leads to destruction. I have known girls who once were on fire for the Lord but took those steps down, and have found it very difficult to get back up. God's gifts and callings are without repentance but sometimes the road back to restoration seems so long and hard that many turn back in discouragement and settle for a mediocre lifestyle rather than pressing all the way through.

A DECISION TO ARISE

The prodigal did some self examination and then he preached to himself. I think it is good to preach to yourself a little! As he preached to himself he received some courage and strength to arise and begin his journey back to his father's house. Maybe some people who are in a back slidden state need to do a little evangelistic work on themselves. Ignore the background noise which comes from the enemy and do as the prodigal. Remember some of the good things which you have received from the Lord in the past. The peace, joy, provisions, protection, fellowship and so much more. The prodigal remembered the food which even the servants ate in abundance and that he was a son. He said "I will get up and go to my father and I will say to him, father I have sinned against heaven and in your sight". This I believe is so beautiful. His rehearsing his speech showed signs of humility. This is what most of us lack. We have been admonished to humble ourselves under the mighty hand of God and He will exalt us in due season. *James 4:10.*

This boy received a total awakening and came to full repentance. The moment he did that, there was a shower of grace made available to him, strengthening him to act in accordance with what he had already been saying. He arose and began his journey back to his father's house. Where sin abounds, grace much more abounds.

The arms of the Father are open wide to embrace you in His love. He will not turn away anyone who is coming to Him in repentance and godly sorrow for sin. "I will greatly rejoice in the Lord, my soul shall be joyful in my God; for He hath clothed me with the garments of salvation, He hath covered me with the robe of righteousness, as a bridegroom decketh himself with ornaments, and as a bride adorneth herself with jewels. *Isaiah 61:10.*

As this boy continued to express his unworthiness and to rehearse his speech of repentance, he felt that if even he could not be accepted as a son he would at least like to be as one of the servants in the house. He still did not quite understand the true heart of his father, and this is what most of us still struggle with when we've been away from God. The struggle is "will He still accept me; I don't feel as a child of God any more; I wonder if He still loves me, I don't know how the brethren will accept me; maybe I will face scorn, shame, censure and rejection."

Nevertheless as he got up and pressed on his journey back to his father something awesome happened. 'But while he was still a long way off, his father saw him and was moved with pity and tenderness for him, and he ran and embraced him and kissed him fervently". *Luke 15:20. AMP. Amplified Bible.*

The father obviously was in great expectation of his son's return. He kept looking for him. In the midst of his breaking heart and tears he continued to hope and to believe that this boy will return home. He had everything ready; the robe of honor, the ring for his hand, sandals for his feet and the wheat fattened calf. Obviously the calf was being nurtured and taken special care of by the servants from it's birth in great anticipation of the father for the celebration of his son's return. The Father sees afar off, while we in our humanity are very near sighted. His heart is one of compassion for those He created for His glory. The Bible says "For thou, Lord, art good, and ready to forgive; and plenteous in mercy unto all them that call upon Thee." Psalm 86:5. Even when Israel sinned and disobeyed Him by provoking Him to anger and jealousy with graven images and idols, causing them to be led into captivity and subjected to their enemies, He had mercy upon them and continued to promise and give them freedom and deliverance so they could follow His plan for them. *Psalm 78:58-72.*

pamela b h victor

RESTORATION

Even though the smell of the pigs was on this young man, due to his wallowing in the mire, he was welcome in his father's arms of love and in his house. The robe reinstated him back into the position of being right with his father from which he had fallen; the ring guaranteed that his covenant relationship was still binding [he was still a son loved by his father and entitled to all that he had, giving him the full rights as a son], and his new sandals, which would differentiate him from a slave which is what he had opted to become.

But the father said to the bond servants "bring quickly the best robe [the festive robe of honor] and put it on him; and give him a ring for his hand and sandals for his feet and bring out that wheat fattened calf and kill it, and let us revel and feast and be happy and make merry." *John 15, Verse 22-23. AMP. Amplified Bible.*

Wow! What a party! Remember that the boy actually wasted his father's inheritance and had nothing left. Not only so but to go near to pigs as much as to feed them and even to eat what they ate must have been one of the greatest dishonor to this father and his household. This was totally repulsive. What a scandalous embarrassment to the family name! I take it that this was a Jewish household where pigs were considered to be unclean.

Well in the father's love and mercy he discounted all ritualistic rules and only clung to the fact that his son returned home.

What a picture of our Heavenly Father, who will not send away any of us who come to Him in repentance. Even when we go away from Him, He still longs for us and believes that we will return. He will not force us for we have our own wills which He gave to us to decide to accept His love and mercy! He is love and love never gives up easily. *Love* is not easily angered, for He is slow to get angry but is of abundant mercy. *Love* continues to hope for all things for *Love* never fails, and God the Father is *Love*. He always patiently waits and is so long suffering not willing for any to perish but for all to come to repentance. What a wonderful and gracious Father He is!

"But his older son was in the field; as he returned and came near the house he heard music and dancing" *Verse 25*. I wonder sometimes why the older brother was in the field working. Didn't they have servants? It would seem as though this son is the picture of one trying to earn his/her own way to the Father's heart by doing good works and not just on faith in His love grace and mercy. A kind of perfectionist spirit! For here he began to list his good deeds. "And having called one of the servant boys to him he began to ask what this meant. And he said to him, "your brother has come, and your father has killed that wheat fattened calf, because he has received him back safe and well". *Verse 26-27.*

106

THE HEART OF THE OLDER BROTHER

Here is where the story gets interesting. "But the elder brother was angry [with deep seated wrath] and resolved not to go in. Then his father came out and began to plead with him. But he answered his father" "look! These many years I have served you and I have never disobeyed your command. Yet you never gave me so much as a little kid, that I might revel and feast with my friends, but when this son of yours arrived, who has devoured your estate with immoral women, you have killed for him that [wheat fattened calf!"] *Verse 28-39. Amplified Bible*

His anger and resentment burned so much within him that it spilled out in his words. He could no longer have referred to him as his brother but as 'this son of yours". It is obvious that he had some inner problems which had to be dealt with. He claimed to be serving the father without rewards. He did not realize that his younger brother in repentance had offered to be a servant as he recognized his own unworthiness and was restored back to sonship and forgiven by his father. The elder brother had sonship also but really never recognized it. He kept trying to gain his father's approval to be a "good son" by good works. He really did not know or understand his father's unconditional love for him. As an older son he rightfully had the blessing to obtain more than his younger brother for that was his due portion as his birthright. But he never accepted it. He thought he had to work for it while all the time it was his freely bestowed by his loving father. The one who broke his father's heart freely received his forgiveness and grace, while the other thought his father was unfair to him and did not recognize his good works. He never accepted his inheritance freely but allowed anger and bitterness to reign in his heart. I believe that it is so very important for all of us in the Body of Christ to recognize and be conscious of the Father's love and mercy. Our brothers and sisters who are returning from the "pigpen" need our prayerful support and love. We must bear one another's burdens and so fulfill the law of Christ. Where sin abounds God's grace much more abounds.

We must be watchful for the spirit of the elder brother and not allow it in our hearts and minds. The instruction which Jesus has left in the Body of Christ is this "brethren, if a person is overtaken in misconduct or sin of any sort, you who are spiritual [who are responsive to and controlled by the Holy Spirit] should set him right and restore and reinstate him, without any sense of superiority and with all gentleness, keeping an attentive eye on yourselves lest you should be tempted also." *Galatians 6:1. Amplified Bible.*

The returning backslider or prodigal who receives mercy and love from God's people should remember not to lose heart or faint if he may have to deal with consequences or the buffeting of the enemy in that particular territory of the battle field. God's promise is "for in due time and at the appointed season we shall reap if we do not loosen and relax our courage and faint." *Galatians 6:9. AMP. Amplified Bible.*

Remember that the law of sowing and reaping will always be in effect as long as the earth remains, so even if consequences result and the road becomes long and difficult filled with regret and discouragement due to wrong choices God is faithful. Jesus carried His cross all the way to Calvary and was crucified for us as He bore the weight of the penalty of our sins. Even if you have terrible things to reap Jesus will never leave you or forsake you.

The point is that just as this young man in the story opted just to serve anywhere in the house, we should also adopt this very same attitude. His humility made room for him to be promoted back to the full rights of a son and not to be on the level of the servants or slaves. God is the one who exalts and promotes us when we humble ourselves in repentance and allow Him to work in our lives shaping and remolding us as He sees fit.

Many run away from this because it involves discipline. But what son is there that his Father does not discipline? We are not bastards but sons and daughters of the Most High God our Father. Some do not want to deal with any type of discipline so they remain on the sidelines only passing through the presence of God once in a while in a worship service but are afraid of God because they still do not recognize Him as their Father. They feel condemned and entertain satan's lies that if they come all the way the road will be too hard. Yes the way of the transgressor is hard, but you must keep pressing through the voice of the enemy's lies until you break completely through, and it is doable. You have the help of the Holy Spirit to strengthen you and to comfort you when you feel weak or cannot go on. Your Father's arms are open to you and He has your restoration healing and deliverance in mind. After all this is what Jesus died to purchase for us all. As you humble yourself and get under some form of spiritual authority and accountability you will have the total victory.

It does not matter what sin you may have fallen into. Whether it is pornography, babies out of wedlock, promiscuity, homosexuality or other abominable acts, all is not lost. All is not lost! There is a new beginning if you will arise and return to your father's house in true repentance.

Satan being judged way back in the Garden to crawl on his belly all the days of his life seeks to draw each person into those low places of degeneracy; but the Hand of the Potter is outstretched now to lift you up and plant you once again into His beautiful Garden through His plan of redemption, regeneration, restoration and renewal. Please let Him, so that He could once again say to the devil "this my son was dead, and is alive again! He was lost but now is found."

In the book of *Jeremiah 18:1-4*. "The word of the Lord which came to Jeremiah from the Lord, "arise and go down to the potter's house, and there I will cause you to hear my words." Then I went down to the potter's house and behold he was working at the wheel. And the vessel that he was making from clay was spoiled in the hand of the potter; so he made it over; reworking it into another vessel as it seemed good to the potter to make it."

God already knows every person's heart. He already knows whether we will fail and fall and has provided in His mercy for this. He knew that Israel would dishonor Him and turn their backs on Him to worship other gods and idols but He never stopped loving them and caring for them, and made plans and provision for their restoration and return to him continually. "O house of Israel, cannot I do with you as this potter? saith the Lord. Behold as the clay is in the potter's hand so are ye in mine hand oh house of Israel." *Verse 6.*

Sometimes He has to make another vessel as it seems fit to him and His use but the clay never decides on this. It is all the work of the Great potter who is well able in His infinite wisdom to remake, remold, and reshape our misshapen lives so that He will still get the most glory in the end. Our duty is to yield to Him and let Him have His way. Remember He said "I know the thoughts that I think toward you, saith the Lord, thoughts of peace and not of evil, to give you an expected end". *Jeremiah 29:11.*

Thank God our sins are forgiven. Doubt and condemnation are shattered, for surely He has forgiven every one of us.

It should be the prayer of every one of us whose lives have been touched by the Lord and have experienced His forgiveness, love, mercy and compassion and restoration in our lives to be always mindful and merciful to the returning backslider who has been to the pigpen. We should remember that if it had not been for the Lord's mercy, we would be in the same or even worst circumstances. Sometimes we tend to forget, but it should be uppermost in our minds always of the deep miry places that the Lord in His mercy has had to rescue some of us from.

The *"elder brother spirit"* is one of criticism, judgementalism, condemnation and self righteousness. This does not help to restore anyone. Remember that those who wandered off into dark places and to the pigpen, have lost their sensitivity to the Father's voice and touch, and the only way for them to be restored is through forgiveness and love demonstrated by the members of His family. Angry stares and raised eyebrows, with cold greetings do not restore anyone. We have been given the ministry of reconciliation in Christ Jesus and must practice it every time. We should always ask the Father by the Holy Spirit to help us to see through His eyes and His heart, so that we carry out His will in allowing people to return in His love and be forgiven. This will eradicate the guilt and shame and make room for godly sorrow as they realize God's mercy and great love. The Apostle Paul even told the church in Corinth one time that they should not leave room for satan by walking in unforgiveness and lack of love to people who sinned and were returning to the fellowship. *2 Corinthians 2:9-11.* He urged them to forgive so as not to allow satan to have an advantage over them. This applies to all of us.

There is a little story in the bible of a blind man who was brought to Jesus. *Mark 8:22-24. King James.* "And he took the blind man by the hand and led him out of the town; and when he had spit on his eyes, and put his hands upon him, He asked him if he saw ought. And he looked up, and said, I see men as trees walking". If we are not careful we could see people like trees and not as God sees them in his love. The next verse goes on to say, "after that He put His hands again upon his eyes, and made him look up; and he was restored and saw everything more clearly." *Verse 25.* Sometimes because we have remained in the House we take a lot for granted and forget God's purpose for people's lives. We can get cold and self consumed in our works in the house and our "own field" as the elder brother of the prodigal, while the souls of men will lose priority in our own eyes. A second touch from Jesus, where the scales will fall from our eyes and the eye salve applied will help us to refocus on God's awesome plan for the restoration and healing of broken, wounded lives.

POEM:

"Who am I that You should call me by your grace and mercy so pure,
And wash and cleanse me so wholly by the blood of Your Son who is Lord.
You have placed me in Your kingdom now to be Your hands Your feet Your all.
I've roamed the whole earth over in places dark and deep. BUT Your mighty Hand sought and found me, to rescue me from certain defeat.
Now I can tell to those who are hurting, that in You I've found a friend,
And that they may embrace this love You offer to give them a future and an expected end."

And may the God of peace [Who is the author and giver of peace], Who brought again from among the dead our Lord Jesus, that great Shepherd of the sheep, by the blood [that sealed, ratified] the everlasting agreement [covenant, testament] strengthen [complete, perfect] and make you what you ought to be and equip you with everything good that you may carry out His will; [while He Himself] works in you and accomplishes that which is pleasing in His sight, through Jesus Christ [the Messiah]; to whom be glory forever and ever [to the ages of the ages] Amen [so be it] Hebrews 13:20-21. Amplified Bible.

If you never asked the Lord Jesus to come into you heart this is your opportunity to pray this prayer: Know that you need a Saviour for you cannot save yourself. Works of self righteousness and religious observances will not give you eternal life nor right standing with God. Jesus Christ paid a tremendous price for your soul, and offers you the only way to heaven, and freedom from sin and eternal death. Pray this prayer by faith and receive Him as you Lord and Saviour.

Dear God, I come to you a sinner. I have broken all your laws and stand in need of forgiveness. I thank you that Jesus paid the price for all my sin on the cross of Calvary and made a way for me to come back to you.

Forgive me of my sins, and wash me in the blood of Jesus.

I open my heart and receive you Lord Jesus. I confess with my mouth that Jesus is Lord and believe in my heart that God has raised Him from the dead.

Come into my heart Lord Jesus and be my Lord and Saviour from this day on.

Make me a brand new creature and change me from the inside out. I thank you and I praise you. *Amen.*

The Holy Spirit comes to live in you as a result of praying this prayer, and you can now ask Jesus to fill and empower you with His Spirit, giving you the experience of the apostles in the book of Acts 2, and according to the admonition of the Apostle Paul to the Christians in the book of Ephesians 5:18. God has given us the gift of the Holy Spirit whom He promised so that we could serve and be the effective witnesses of His resurrection as we ought to be.